THE PURGE OF JAPANESE LEADERS UNDER THE OCCUPATION

BY

HANS H. BAERWALD

UNIVERSITY OF CALIFORNIA PUBLICATIONS IN POLITICAL SCIENCE
Volume 8

UNIVERSITY OF CALIFORNIA PRESS
BERKELEY AND LOS ANGELES
1959

UNIVERSITY OF CALIFORNIA PUBLICATIONS IN POLITICAL SCIENCE

VOLUME VIII

THE PURGE OF JAPANESE LEADERS UNDER THE OCCUPATION

BY

HANS H. BAERWALD

UNIVERSITY OF CALIFORNIA PRESS
BERKELEY AND LOS ANGELES
1959

University of California Publications in Political Science
Editors (Berkeley): George Lenczowski, E. B. Haas

Volume 8

Submitted by editors March 10, 1958
Issued November 3, 1959
Price, $2.25

University of California Press
Berkeley and Los Angeles
California

Cambridge University Press
London, England

PRINTED IN THE UNITED STATES OF AMERICA

FOR DIANE

ACKNOWLEDGMENTS

This study was made possible by a Foreign Study and Research Fellowship from the Ford Foundation. Without the generous financial assistance and general encouragement extended by the Foundation and its officers, I would not have been able to spend eighteen months in Japan in 1954 and 1955 gathering material for this study and reassessing the purge in its many facets. It is incumbent upon me to add, however, that the Ford Foundation and its officers are not responsible for the data presented and the personal views expressed in these pages.

I would not have applied for a research grant from the Ford Foundation and certainly would not have received it, had it not been for the support of my mentors in the Department of Political Science at the University of California in Berkeley. I owe a particular debt of gratitude to Professor Robert A. Scalapino who was unfailing in his encouragement. For like reasons, I wish to thank Professors Leslie Lipson and Ernest Haas who steered the manuscript through the process of readying it for publication. Professor Delmer Brown of the Department of History at the University of California had much to do with developing my academic interest in Japan and its people.

The many friends and acquaintances in Japan who assisted me in my labors are too numerous to mention. Since the subject matter remains politically controversial to this day, it is possible that I would be doing them a disservice by mentioning them individually. Our stay in Japan was made comfortable for my family and myself only by the efforts of Donald and Barbara Helm whose assistance was in the grand tradition of friendship.

I also gratefully acknowledge the financial assistance from Miami University's Alumni Loyalty Fund which made it possible for me to send a fresh manuscript to the publisher.

In conclusion, I can only say that my wife contributed more than the usual wifely share to make sure that what follows would see the light of day and that its preparation would be enjoyable as well. It is to her that this volume is dedicated.

H. H. B.

Oxford, Ohio
November, 1958

CONTENTS

Chapter I

INTRODUCTION

During the early years of the Occupation, Japan was the scene of an attempt to alter the political, economic, and social framework of a nation. This effort is often referred to as Japan's "democratization" and was among the terms of surrender acceded to by its leaders in the cessation of hostilities. Envisaged in the policy documents which were to serve as guidelines for the Occupation were reforms which ranged from rewriting the organic law, through restructuring the economic system in both its industrial and agricultural components, to inducing changes in that most intimate of human relations—the family.

The task of reforming Japan in the early period of the Occupation has all too often been overshadowed by the demilitarization program. However, during the reform stages of the Occupation, Japan also served as a laboratory in which western ideas, institutions, and methods were tested within the context of an Asian society. It is hoped that an analysis of the successes and failures of one aspect of this reform effort will provide some insight into the process of attempting the forcible and manipulated transformation of one society by another.

This kind of radical transformation—we might even term it a revolution—is complicated and difficult even when undertaken by the citizens of the society itself. The problems are compounded when, as in the Occupation of Japan, the transformation is directed by forces foreign to the society. Destruction of the controlled society's fabric could probably be accomplished with relative ease. More difficult would be the task of rebuilding the society along lines alien to its traditions. The compromise made between the objectives of the Occupation and the realities encountered in Japan serves as one focus for the material in this study.

Within this broad context, the Occupation program with which we are specifically concerned is officially entitled "The Removal and Exclusion of Undesirable Personnel from Public Office." More popularly known as the "Purge," this program was the Occupation's principal tool for transforming Japan's political leadership.

What were the objectives of the purge? The answer seems deceptively simple if phrased as the elimination of "undesirable personnel" from Japan's reservoir of political talent. However, defining categories of persons whose leadership would be inimical to the new Japan proved difficult. In fact, much of the material which follows attempts to trace the tortuous path toward determination of categories of undesirable persons. Much of the difficulty lay in the confusion surrounding the exact delineation of the ultimate aims of the purge.

The purge was initially conceived as a phase of the demilitarization program in terms of which individuals would be removed from office if the peace of the world would be endangered by their remaining in positions of political power. But quite early in the Occupation, the purge program became associated with the democratization effort (albeit in a negative manner) so that it became the vehicle for removing from office any persons deemed inimical to the growth of democracy in Japan. The confusion over the objectives of the purge was compounded by the over-all shift in Occupation policy from one which emphasized Japan's democratization to one which stressed making Japan a bulwark of stability in the revolution sweeping through Asia. This lack of clarity in the objectives of the purge and the over-all shift in Occupation policy are best reflected in the criteria on the basis of which purge designations were made. Hence it is the policy-making process in relation to the purge criteria which serves as a second focus for the empirical data collected.

Attention is thereupon given to problems encountered in the purge's administrative implementation. An initial question was whether administrative or judicial procedures should be used in the designation of purgees. To this problem was added the question of how much independence was to be granted to the Japanese government in executing the purge, and conversely, how much supervision the Occupation was to exercise over the process of implementing the program. Underlying these problems was the dilemma posed by the need for the effective implementation of Occupation objectives and the necessity that the reforms undertaken should be carried out by the Japanese administrators themselves. The discussion of these problems rests on the assumption that even the most clearly defined policy—and the purge was not one—is dependent for its success on the adequacy of the mechanism through which it is executed.

The problem of reconciling means with ends lies at the heart of the difficulties encountered in carrying out the purge. This hypothetical relation rests on two assumptions: first, that the Occupation was taking seriously its objective of "democratizing" Japan; and that one of the fundamental theories which the Occupation was trying to transplant was the Anglo-Saxon concept of "due process of the law." Nowhere were the strains and stresses involved in this dual effort better exemplified than in the administration of the purge. Once the purge criteria were fully formulated, it proved to be relatively easy to designate those deemed undesirable. But problems of a more subtle nature had to be faced once the issue was raised of restricting the political activities of those designated. When the administrators of the purge turned their attention to the surveillance of the purgees, the specter of totalitarian controls reappeared as an important element in Japanese politics.

In assessing the impact of the purge on the dominant power groups in Japanese society, answers can be found to two basic questions. Since the removal of those who had deceived and misled the people of Japan to embark on world conquest had been the original objective, it follows that the persons purged would represent the American view of who was to blame. As soon as the Occupation added to the original terms of reference set for the purge the objective of removing those leaders deemed inimical to the growth of democracy, the persons purged under this category would in effect be defined as being antidemocrats. In the course of this analysis some insight is also gained into the image held by the Occupation of the ideal leaders who were to rule the new and democratic Japan.

In restricting the assessment of the purge's impact to these questions, only limited attention is devoted to assaying the influence of the purge on present political developments. Although certain tentative conclusions are set forth, I believe it premature to hazard such an analysis.[1]

Two questions are posed in the conclusion. Was the purge, as employed by the Occupation in Japan, efficacious as a technique in reconstituting and reorienting the political leadership of that society? Can the techniques employed in a program comparable to the purge be reconciled with the objective of establishing the political framework of a liberal democratic society? The answer to this last question becomes crucial if consideration is given to the possibility of utilizing the purge technique in other societies that are in the midst of rapid social, economic, and technological change. Societies undertaking such a transformation also face the problem of how to deal with an established leadership standing in opposition to such change. More important are

[1] An analysis of the purge in this context awaits a fully integrated survey of the total impact made on the people of Japan and their social, political, and economic institutions by the experience of the Occupation and the reform programs which were attempted.

the problems of finding and elevating to positions of power new leaders dedicated to the process of change. The purge tried to face up to these problems, although it did so in a hesitant and ambivalent manner. Its basic philosophy ultimately rested on the assumption that a leadership had to be found which was committed to accept liberal democratic values before the establishment of an economic, political, and social milieu within which such a leadership could grow in the western world.

CHAPTER II

OBJECTIVES OF THE PURGE

THE POTSDAM DECLARATION set forth the terms of surrender and the over-all objectives which the victors wished to accomplish in Japan during the period of Occupation. Paragraph 6 of this Declaration stated, "There must be eliminated for all time the authority and influence of those who have deceived and misled the people of Japan into embarking on world conquest, for we insist that a new order of peace, security and justice will be impossible until irresponsible militarism is driven from the world."[1] Several interesting assumptions underlie this objective. First, the Japanese people were "deceived and misled" into embarking on world conquest, which implies that leadership played a predominant role. Second, "irresponsible militarism" constituted the most significant factor obstructing the peace of the world. This view is reinforced in another paragraph of the Declaration agreed upon by the heads of the governments of the United States, the United Kingdom, and China. Japan's choice in accepting surrender is couched within the alternatives of: (1) continuing to be controlled by "self-willed militaristic advisers, whose unintelligent calculations have brought the Empire of Japan to the threshold of annihilation," or (2) "following the path of reason."[2] To recapitulate: Japan's leader-

[1] Paragraph 6 of the Potsdam Declaration, a proclamation signed by the President of the United States, the Prime Minister of the United Kingdom, and concurred in by dispatch by the President of the National Government of China. Text is from *Political Reorientation of Japan, September 1945 to September 1948* (hereafter cited as *PRJ*), p. 413. The exact origin of this paragraph of the Potsdam Declaration is as yet not established. In his memoirs, *Turbulent Era: A Diplomatic Record of Forty Years,* Joseph C. Grew indicates on page 1431 that a memorandum setting forth most of the content of the Potsdam Declaration was prepared under his direction in the state department during May, 1945. The draft proclamation (pp. 1431 to 1434) as a whole bears a close resemblance to the final product, and the paragraph which became the sixth of the Proclamation is, in its essentials, in final form. In Henry L. Stimson's memoirs, *On Active Service in Peace and War,* the draft proclamation is referred to as the "Stimson Memorandum" (pp. 620–624). Both would seem to be correct. The then Undersecretary of State Grew, no doubt, did have a large share in the writing of the original draft. Since he did not attend the Potsdam Conference, and as the then Secretary of War Stimson did, it probably became the "Stimson Memorandum" for the conference sessions. Of interest is that neither of the memoirs alludes to any controversy having surrounded this particular paragraph. This view is further substantiated by former President Truman's *Memoirs: Vol. I, Year of Decisions,* pp. 390–392, and in James F. Byrnes' *Speaking Frankly,* pp. 207–214, by their not referring to this particular paragraph as having been discussed at any great length. In all instances, the central problem is the disposition of the emperor.

[2] Paragraph 4 of the Potsdam Declaration.

ship, swayed by the siren song of irresponsible militarism, had deceived and misled the people, guiding them initially on a path of world conquest and thence to the brink of annihilation. This analysis contains the germ of far-reaching hypotheses concerning the structure of Japanese society and the causes of World War II.[3] More important, however, is the attention lavished on the twin factors of leadership and irresponsible militarism in the basic document setting forth the Occupation's objectives.

The authority and influence of this leadership were not only to be eliminated, but were to be eliminated for all time. We cannot but wonder if the formulators of this paragraph realized its scope. Its inclusiveness becomes apparent when we examine the interpretations which set out the specific objectives in detail. Two directives provided these more specific aims. One directive came from the State, War, Navy Coordinating Committee (hereafter SWNCC) in September, 1945;[4] the other directive was issued by the Joint Chiefs of Staff (hereafter JCS) in November.[5] Both of these agencies were United States government institutions. The Moscow Foreign Ministers Conference held in December of that year envisaged multinational control and policy formulation to be exercised through the eleven-member Far Eastern Commission[6] and the four-member Allied Council for Japan. But because these previous instructions, issued only as interim directives, were not overruled by the Far Eastern Commission, they came to acquire international legal status.[7] Hence it was United States govern-

[3] These hypotheses can be readily questioned. To do so, however, would involve amassing a mountain of evidence and analysis detailing the complex interaction of the internal workings of the Japanese government and the society it controlled, as well as their relationship to international developments.

[4] "United States Initial Post-Surrender Policy for Japan" (hereafter cited as SWNCC Directive). For text, cf. *PRJ*, Vol. II, pp. 423–426.

[5] "Basic Initial Post-Surrender Directive to Supreme Commander for the Allied Powers for the Occupation and Control of Japan" (hereafter cited as JCS Directive). For text, cf. *PRJ*, Vol. II, pp. 428–439.

[6] A predecessor of this agency was the Far Eastern Advisory Commission. For full text of the December 27, 1945, Moscow Agreement establishing the Far Eastern Commission, cf. *PRJ*, Vol. II, pp. 421–422.

[7] Far Eastern Commission, Press Release No. 34, July 10, 1947. It reported that the Commission had unanimously adopted the Basic Post-Surrender Policy for Japan on June 19, 1947. This policy statement included the following: "The restoration, even in a disguised form, of any anti-democratic and militaristic activity shall be prevented, particularly on the part of former Japanese career military and naval officers, gendarmerie, and former members of dissolved militaristic, ultranationalistic, and other anti-democratic organizations. . . . Obstacles to the revival and strengthening of democratic tendencies among the Japanese people shall be removed" (p. 4). The reader is requested to note the apparent equation of "anti-democratic" with "militaristic" activity. Had the formulators been concerned with differentiating the two types of proscribed activity, the plural would have been appropriate.

ment institutions which set forth in detailed form the basic policies of the purge.

A dichotomy of objectives is apparent in the SWNCC and JCS directives. On the one hand there is expressed the aim of creating a Japan that "will not again become a menace . . . to the peace and security of the world." In line with this aim, "Japan will be completely disarmed and demilitarized. The authority of the militarists and the influence of militarism will be totally eliminated from her political, economic, and social life. Institutions expressive of the spirit of militarism and aggression will be vigorously suppressed."[8] To carry out these aims, it was directed that:

> High officials of the Japanese Imperial General Staff, other high military and naval officials of the Japanese Government, and other important exponents of militarism and aggression will be taken into custody and held for future disposition. Persons who have been active exponents of militarism and militant nationalism will be removed and excluded from public office and from any other positions of public or substantial private responsibility. Ultra-nationalistic or militaristic social, political, professional and commercial societies and institutions will be dissolved and prohibited.[9]

The JCS directive went one step further in ordering that specified categories of individuals were to be arrested and held as suspected war criminals.

> 1. All members of the Supreme Military Council, the Board of Field Marshals and Fleet Admirals, the Imperial General Headquarters, and the Army and Navy General Staff.
>
> 2. All commissioned officers of the Gendarmerie (Kempei), and all officers of the Army and Navy who have been important exponents of militant nationalism and aggression.
>
> 3. All key members of ultranationalistic, terroristic, and secret patriotic societies, and
>
> 4. All persons who you have reason to believe are war criminals or whose names or descriptions are contained in lists of suspected war criminals which have been or may be furnished to you.
>
> 5. All persons who have played an active and dominant governmental, economic, financial, or other significant part in the formulation or execution of Japan's program of aggression and all high officials of the Political Association of Great Japan, the Imperial Rule Assistance Association, the Imperial Rule Assistance Political

[8] SWNCC Directive, Part I, "Ultimate Objectives," paragraph b. *PRJ*, Vol. II, p. 423.

[9] SWNCC Directive, Part III, "Political," paragraph 1, "Disarmament and Demilitarization." *PRJ*, Vol. II, p. 424. The directive also noted that military influence in the schools, both in training and in personnel, should be removed. The program implementing this part of the directive, known as the "educational purge," did not become a part of the so-called "political purge."

Society and their agencies and affiliates or successor organizations will be interned pending further disposition. You may intern other civilians as necessary for the achievement of your mission.[10]

Only a very small minority of individuals in these categories were incarcerated and tried as war criminals. In reality, it was the purge which implemented these parts of the SWNCC and JCS directives.

Fostering of democratic ideals and institutions constitutes the other part of the dichotomy of objectives present in these policy statements. "The Japanese people shall be encouraged to develop a desire for individual liberties and respect for fundamental human rights, particularly the freedoms of religion, assembly, speech, and the press. They shall also be encouraged to form democratic and representative organizations."[11] The JCS directive gave further body to prior instructions:

Subject to the necessity of maintaining the security of the occupying forces, the formation and activities of democratic political parties with rights of assembly and public discussion will be encouraged. Free elections of representative local government should be held at the earliest practicable date, and at the regional and national levels as directed, after consideration of your recommendations, through the Joint Chiefs of Staff. Your action in connection with the program referred to in this subparagraph should be taken in the light of one of the ultimate objectives of the occupation, the establishment, in accordance with the freely expressed will of the Japanese people, of a peacefully inclined and responsible government.[12]

A two-pronged effort is envisaged in these policy statements. First is the destruction of Japan's war-making potential. The purge of Japan's wartime leadership is generally classified as belonging within this, the first objective. By removing this leadership, another step would be taken toward Japan's pacification. A new dimension was thereby added to traditional theories analyzing causes of war. Leadership is placed alongside economic, social, historical, and military pressures. In fact, what emerges is the belief that an elite imposes its will on objective forces as opposed to being guided by them. Man's fate is self-determined. This philosophy of human behavior may be a necessary prerequisite for democratic theory. That it is adequate as an analysis of the reasons why the Japanese people went to war is open to question. Whatever position we take on the validity of this analysis, one objective of the purge clearly emerges—namely, that it was to eliminate the leadership potential in Japan's capacity to wage war.

[10] JCS Directive, Part I, "General and Political," paragraph 7. *PRJ*, Vol. II, pp. 431–432.

[11] SWNCC Directive, Part I, "Ultimate Objectives," paragraph c. *PRJ*, Vol. II, p. 423.

[12] JCS Directive, Part I, "General and Political," paragraph 9, subparagraph c. *PRJ*, Vol. II, p. 433.

A second objective emerges from these policy statements. This is the rebuilding of Japanese society on the basis of ideals most commonly associated with liberal democracy. The germ of this conception can be noted in the SWNCC and JCS policy papers wherein the destructive rather than constructive aspects of occupation objectives aimed at creating a new society are stressed. On the issuance of the purge directive[13] an official press release set forth its objectives, as being "to strike the shackles from the efforts of the Japanese people to rise toward freedom and democracy."[14] Furthermore, the official account of the implementation of the purge contains the unequivocal statement that "the basic philosophy of the purge program was that it should be a means of creating a new democratic leadership responsive to the will of the people."[15] The full potentialities of viewing the purge in the light of this objective become clear when the reasons for directing the purge against the leadership of the Communist party of Japan are noted.

> The guiding philosophy of this phase [i.e., the removal of obstacles to the strengthening of democratic tendencies among the Japanese people] of the Occupation has been preventive, not punitive. Its purpose and effect have been to provide that the aims of Allied policy in the democratization of Japan would not be thwarted by the influence and pressure of *anti-democratic elements.* The area of its application for the most part has embraced those persons who because of position and influence bear responsibility for Japan's totalitarian policies which led to adventure in conquest and exploitation. Recently, however, a new and no less sinister groupment [i.e., the Communist Party] has injected itself into the Japanese political scene which has sought through perversion of truth and incitation to mass violence to transform this peaceful and tranquil island into an arena of disorder and strife as the means of stemming Japan's notable progress along the road of representative democracy and to subvert the rapidly growing democratic tendencies among the Japanese people.[16]

To be sure, this view of the purge's objectives was not voiced until four years and a half after its inception. Sufficient evidence is presented, however, to indicate that the objective of expulsion of antidemocratic elements from Japan's leadership could be noted in early policy statements.

---

[13] "Removal and Exclusion of Undesirable Personnel from Public Office," SCAPIN 550. *PRJ*, Vol. II, pp. 482–488.

[14] Supreme Commander for the Allied Powers, Press Release, January 4, 1946. *PRJ*, Vol. I, p. 45.

[15] "Removal of Ultranationalists," *PRJ*, Vol. I, p. 45.

[16] General Douglas MacArthur, "Letter to Prime Minister Yoshida," June 6, 1950. SCAP Press Release. For background data and partial text of letter, cf. Major General Courtney Whitney, *MacArthur, His Rendezvous with History*, p. 310.

It is my thesis that much of the acrimonious controversy which surrounds the purge even today stems from this confusion concerning its basic objectives. To remove individuals from authority and influence in public affairs for having been "tainted with war responsibility" is one thing. To do so because they are or may become antidemocratic is to introduce a plethora of new factors. So long as the first objective remained primary, the purge was solidly based. As soon as the second objective came to be emphasized, the entire objective of the purge became ambiguous. It is assumed that democracy is a concept having a definition so crystal-clear that its supporters and its antagonists can be readily determined. Yet there could and did occur cases in which individual leaders who had worked within the parliamentary part of Japan's pre-World War II government had actively supported Japan's policy of militant aggression. Since "parliamentarism," however, is generally equated with democratic institutions and behavior, the individuals who had confined their activities within this rubric could logically claim to have acted democratically and hence should not be subjected to the purge. Other individuals among Japan's leaders could be found who had opposed the aggressively expansionist policies, but who were nonetheless strong believers in theories propounding the primacy of the state over the individual. Quite a number of the members of the bureaucracy fit into this category. These individuals certainly should have been purged if the objective was to remove antidemocrats, yet they were rarely touched by the criteria setting up specific categories.

The crux of the problem can be summarized as follows: The original objective was to remove leaders whose past activities indicated that to leave them in positions of power and influence would endanger the peace of the world. To this was added General MacArthur's concept that the objective of the purge was to remove antidemocrats with the hope that by removing these individuals, "democratic leadership responsive to the will of the people" would be fostered. In the final analysis, "pro-expansionists" were equated with "anti-democrats," and "anti-expansionists" with "pro-democrats." This confusion of objectives and of identifications led to a number of complex problems in defining the purge criteria. For example, it makes a considerable difference whether the categories of purge criteria are formulated on the basis of covering those officials who were responsible for Japan's military aggression, or removing those whose retention in positions of authority and influence would be inimical to the growth of democracy in Japan. I believe that the most serious defect of the purge was the incompatibility of its basic objectives. From this incompatibility flowed numerous objections to the purge which foreign observers, as well as Japanese, have made. Furthermore, results that could have been achieved by the purge were delineated by these objectives and the criteria implementing them.

CHAPTER III

EVOLUTION OF CRITERIA

TWO CATEGORIES of criteria constitute the heart of the purge program. The first category defines those positions which are to be classified as entailing sufficient authority and influence to warrant that purgees not be permitted to hold them. On the surface, defining this category would seem to be a simple process. For example, all elective positions, all positions in the governmental bureaucracy, important posts in political parties, and the like would be included. However, these examples of "public office" which came to be the technical term for "positions of authority and influence" (the phrase of the Potsdam Declaration) are far from complete. To mention just one important group, principal officials in the industrial and business combines are not included.

The second category of criteria defines those positions which were sufficiently important in the pre-surrender imperial Japanese government and within the framework of Japanese society for their occupants to be designated as purgees. The SWNCC and JCS directives provide a list of major groups which were to be included in the latter category: the military and certain specified groups within the armed forces such as the kempeitai (gendarmerie), leaders of ultranationalistic organizations, leaders of the Imperial Rule Assistance Association and its affiliates, and the general phrase "persons who have played an active and dominant governmental, economic, financial or other significant part in the formulation or execution of Japan's program of aggression."[1] The last clause could cover a very large category, depending upon its interpretation.

One confusion that often can be noted in comments concerning the purge, is that no distinction is made between these two categories. Two sets of criteria had to be worked out: criteria for positions of authority and influence from which purgees were to be excluded, and criteria on the basis of which groups of individuals (or occasionally individuals) were to be designated as purgees. Confusion surrounding this distinction is readily understandable in that it even included one high Occupation official who had helped to draft the purge directive. "The cleansing directive requires the Japanese Government to institute a program of removal of officials of the national and prefectural governments (of *Shinnin* and *Chokunin* ranks) and to bar from re-

[1] JCS Directive, Part I, "General and Political," paragraph 7. *PRJ*, Vol. II, p. 432.

appointment to any government office any person who falls within specified categories."[2] This statement implies that all government officials who held *Chokunin* and *Shinnin* ranks were to be removed. In actuality, this group of officials belonged in the first-named category and only if they fell under purge criteria were they subject to removal.[3]

The Problem of Responsibility

A certain assumption is implicit in the differentiation between those who held positions of authority and those who did not, that is, the assumption that position, authority, and power could be equated. The Occupation, however, chose not to recognize this equation in the case of the emperor as an individual and of his position as the keystone in the arch of the imperial Japanese government of the prewar and wartime era. As is well known, the emperor was neither tried as a war criminal nor subjected to the purge. Many complex factors went into the decision not to touch the emperor.[4] Foremost among these was the belief that the convenience of the Occupation would be served by his retention. Acceptance of the Occupation was to be channeled through the emperor. This decision was one facet of the over-all policy to work through the existing governmental structure and the officials manning it. An alternative approach to that employed in the purge was used to reduce the emperor's power. The 1947 Constitution relegated him to being "the symbol of the State and of the unity of the people."[5] Under the Meiji Constitution, by contrast, he had been "the head of the Empire, combining in Himself the rights of sovereignty."[6]

On the issue of his role in Japan's war effort, the emperor at one point did state, "I come to you, General MacArthur, to offer myself to

[2] *Report of Government Section to Far Eastern Commission,* p. 12. Japan's civil service, before Occupation reforms, was classified according to the following ranks: *Shinnin,* who were appointed by a decree bearing the personal seal of the emperor in addition to the imperial seal, and signed by the prime minister. This rank was restricted to cabinet ministers, privy councilors, ambassadors and vice-ministers. *Chokunin,* who were appointed by a decree bearing the imperial seal countersigned by the prime minister. This rank was held by the top three grades of the higher civil service (*Kōtō-Kan*). *Sonin,* who were appointed by a decree bearing the seal of the Privy Council. This rank was held by the other seven grades of the higher civil service, entrance to which was dependent on passing the *Kōtō Bunkan Shiken* (higher civil service examination). *Hannin,* who were appointed by the respective cabinet ministers. Of inferior rank, they were divided into five classes.

[3] SCAPIN 550, paragraph 3 a, b. *PRJ,* Vol. II, p. 482.

[4] The complete story behind this decision in itself is worthy as a thesis topic. Cf. Joseph C. Grew, *Turbulent Era,* pp. 1406–1442. Cf. also Major General Courtney Whitney, *MacArthur: His Rendezvous with History,* pp. 238–286.

[5] "The Constitution of Japan" (of 1947), chap. I, Art. I. For text cf. *PRJ,* Vol. II, p. 671.

[6] "The Constitution of the Empire of Japan" (1889, the Meiji Constitution), chap. I, Art. 4. For text cf. *PRJ,* Vol. II, p. 586.

the judgment of the Powers you represent as the one to bear sole responsibility for every political and military decision made and action taken by my people in the conduct of the war."[7] Possibly he should have been taken at his word. The decision not to accept the emperor's assessment of his rôle in the war effort of Japan, regardless of the motivations which induced him to make it, fundamentally compromised the whole effort of removing those who had deceived and misled the Japanese people.

On the other hand, there were many arguments to support the retention of the emperor; the task of the Occupation was made easier;[8] and amidst the chaos of a lost war and the radical changes in Japanese society contemplated by the Occupation, it allowed the Japanese people to retain a sense of equilibrium by the continued presence of the father image.[9] Acceptance of these views has as its premise that tranquillity and psychological feelings of security were among the primary objectives of the Occupation. Eventually these views did come to play an important role in guiding policy decisions. However, so far as the SWNCC and JCS policy statements which set forth the objectives of the purge were concerned, social change of revolutionary proportions had been intended.

If passing the buck is the favorite pastime of public or private officialdom, Japan's military, civilian, and industrial bureaucrats are no exception. Formally, the flow of responsibility began and ended with the emperor. In his case this strict construction of the focus of responsibility was ignored. We can argue that he had been merely a robot, manipulated by the holders of real power, and hence not really responsible.[10] However, this line of reasoning can also be applied to a significantly large group of leaders among the elite which had guided Japan's destiny. Observe, for example, answers given by former Prime Minister Shidehara Kijuro to the following questions:

Question: In your affidavit you state as follows: "that action of some kind was contemplated by the military clique." Do you or do you not intend to include Minami [War Minister at the time, regarding whom Shidehara is being questioned] in this terminology?

Shidehara: By "military clique" I did not intend to include General Minami.

[7] Whitney, *op. cit.*, p. 286.

[8] *Ibid.*, pp. 283–286. In these pages General Whitney analyzes some of the basic considerations which motivated General MacArthur in retaining the emperor.

[9] Kyogoku Junichi and Masumi Junnosuke, *Japanese Politics: Is it Democratized?* pp. 18–19.

[10] Maruyama Masao, "Gunkoku Shihaisha no Seishin Keitai" (The Spiritual Structure of Military Leaders), *Choryu* (*Current*), May, 1949, pp. 15–37.

Question: Well, will you explain to the Tribunal whom you intended to include in these words "military clique"?

Shidehara: At the time I heard that it was the younger officers in the Army who were contemplating this action and probably General Minami as War Minister was occupied in keeping order among these younger officers; but I do not know just exactly the names of these younger officers.

Question: Now is it not a fact that the Cabinet has no direct control of the action of the Army as it is not in their jurisdiction?

Shidehara: That is my understanding, that is to say, the Cabinet has no direct voice in Army affairs.

Question: Who in the Cabinet . . . is responsible for the actions and conduct of the Army?

Shidehara: Legally, there is no rule definitely stating who is responsible for this. Therefore I must give my own personal opinion. It is my opinion that the War Minister is responsible, because he is the only one that could be responsible.[11]

Hence, General Minami, too, could claim that he had followed policies because of pressure from his subordinates, or in effect, that he, too, had been a manipulated robot. Yet in the view of a business leader, it had been the military as a whole that had directed the destiny of Japan. Mr. Hatta, former president of the North China Development Company, is answering questions concerning who controlled policies with respect to the need for militarily occupying North China in order to consolidate Japanese trade activities in the area:

Question: Who made this policy?

Mr. Hatta: From the time of the Manchurian Incident the military took charge of policy. A momentum was set up which carried their policy through. The business leaders had to follow. At best they could retard it.

Question: But who made the decisions?

Answer: The Army. But who is the center of the Army? Nobody knows. It was like a current flowing through a large number of young officers in the Army.[12]

No one, it seems, bore responsibility. Yet in order to comply with the Potsdam Declaration, the purge criteria had to be formulated with the objective of removing those who had "deceived and misled the Japanese people to embark on world conquest." This meant that the criteria should include those who had borne a share in the responsibility for this policy. By not including the emperor, the task of justifying the inclusion of this or that position as signifying that its holder bore responsibility became almost impossible. Almost anyone could argue that although he had formally been, for example, a cabinet minister, in reality he had not exercised any of the real power of that position.[13]

[11] International Military Tribunal for the Far East, *Proceedings,* p. 1335.

[12] Jerome B. Cohen, *Japan's Economy in War and Reconstruction,* p. 44.

[13] Most of the appeals from purge designation attempted to prove this point.

The purge, it will be recalled, had two objectives. These were conveniently combined by General MacArthur. "In his mind, the primary purpose of this phase of the Occupation, i.e., the purge, was the removal of leadership tainted with war responsibility from the political, economic, and social life of Japan—that under a new leadership not so tainted, *democratic growth might be possible.*"[14] (Italics mine.) New leaders were to guide Japan. Their only qualification was not to have been associated with the *ancien régime.* Hence, purgees should be judged on the extent of their identification with the prewar and wartime government of Japan. Their "responsibility" for Japan's policy of aggression would become secondary to their having the potential to lead Japan onto the paths of democracy. If this view of the objectives of the purge is accepted, the criteria emerge as guidelines indicating who would be unacceptable as leaders for the new Japan. Furthermore, assuming that clear distinctions may be drawn between protagonists and antagonists of "democracy," this is the only framework within which the criteria could be made reasonable. As noted earlier, this confusion of objectives is believed central to the purge.

Two factors guided the formulation of the purge criteria. First, a certain position in public life (except the emperor's) was considered as prima facie evidence that its holder was responsible for presurrender policies of Japan. Second was the assumption that the individual concerned, regardless of his position, had been an active exponent of policies relating to Japan's embarkation on a war of world conquest. Both factors clearly reflected the intent of the Potsdam Declaration. They did not, however, necessarily reflect MacArthur's objective that the purge would remove those who might impede the democratization of Japan.

Establishing the Categories

Who were to be purged? Seven categories of criteria answered this question.[15] The first tied the purge to the war crimes trials conducted by the International Military Tribunal for the Far East—all "persons arrested as suspected war criminals unless released or acquitted."[16] The second made all career officers of the Imperial Japanese Army and Navy subject to the purge. An initial draft of this category had proposed that only officers of the rank of major or above should automatically be purged. One of the GHQ staff sections, in its comment

[14] "Removal of Ultranationalists," *PRJ,* Vol. I, p. 45.
[15] SCAPIN 550, Appendix "A." *PRJ,* Vol. II, pp. 484–485.
[16] SCAPIN 550, Appendix "A," Category A. *PRJ,* Vol. II, p. 484.

on this category, had even recommended that it be limited to general and flag officers. However, the chief of counter-intelligence, in his comment on the draft, stated that if the directive were to remove only the general and flag officers, it ". . . would eliminate only a very few older men from the public life of the country. In no way would it eliminate the militaristic or ultranationalistic influence of the Army or Navy. . . ." In conclusion, he noted that by so restricting the application of the purge, ". . . It would permit Army and Navy field grade officers to dominate a large section of Japanese life and be elected to public office. . . ."[17] The latter recommendation prevailed and the office of Chief of Staff decided that the JCS directive should be implemented literally. This implementation was not based on the view that all career officers had deceived and misled the people of Japan. To equate the power of General Tojo with second-lieutenant Suzuki, graduate of the Japanese military academy in the summer of 1944, would be patently absurd. The all-inclusive category was based instead on the elimination of the influence of the army and navy.

The third and fourth categories were designed to remove leaders and influential members of "ultranationalistic, terroristic, or secret patriotic societies" as well as those of the Imperial Rule Assistance Association and its affiliates. These categories were based on the following instructions from the Joint Chiefs of Staff.

> Throughout Japan, you [SCAP] will assure the dissolution of the Political Association of Great Japan, the Imperial Rule Assistance Association (*Taisei Yokusan Kai*), the Imperial Rule Assistance Political Society (*Taisei Seijikai*), their affiliates and agencies or any successor organizations, and all Japanese ultranationalistic, terroristic and secret patriotic societies and their agencies and affiliates.[18]

Two directives to the Japanese government implemented this paragraph. One was the purge directive, formally entitled, "Removal and Exclusion of Undesirable Personnel from Public Office."[19] Its companion, issued on the same day, was named "Abolition of Certain Political Parties, Associations, Societies, and Other Organizations."[20] The latter directive had as its aim the dissolution of these societies, whereas the former made its leaders subject to the purge. Neither the Imperial

[17] Memorandum is quoted on p. 11 of "History of the Purge" (unpublished Government Section draft of "Removal of Ultranationalists," in *PRJ*, Vol. I).

[18] JCS Directive, Part I, "General and Political," paragraph 5, "Political and Administrative Reorganization," subparagraph g, *PRJ*, Vol. II, p. 431.

[19] SCAPIN 550. For full text, cf. *PRJ*, Vol. II, pp. 482–488.

[20] SCAPIN 548. For full text, cf. *PRJ*, Vol. II, pp. 479–481.

Rule Assistance Association (IRAA)[21] nor any of its affiliates was ever formally dissolved under the terms of SCAPIN 548. Only by formally designating them for abolition, however, would the sanctions of the latter directive be applicable, that is, impounding of the property of the organization and designation of officials down to and including "influential members" as purgees. A compromise was thus effected. Formal dissolution and its sanctions were applied against the ultranationalistic, secret, and terroristic societies. Against the Imperial Rule organizations, such steps were not taken. Instead, a special category listing only certain positions of leadership in these associations was established. This compromise is indicative of the measures employed to maintain a balance between what higher policy directed and what the exigencies of the situation dictated. To apply the purge down to the influential member level of the Imperial Rule organizations would have cut a deep swath into the political leadership resources of Japan.

It is interesting to note that the same pattern of action was taken at a later date against another political organization. SCAPIN 548, in establishing criteria for dissolution of organizations, encompassed those whose purpose included "Resistance or opposition to the Occupation Forces . . ." as well as "Alteration of policy by . . . terroristic programs. . . ."[22] These criteria were used as the basis for purging the top leadership of the Communist party of Japan in the summer of 1950. In support of the "terroristic" activities engaged in by party members, two instances were cited. One was the so-called "Eels incident" in which leftist-inspired students of Tohoku University booed an educational officer attached to the Civil Information and Education Section (GHQ, SCAP) during the course of a speech. The second was the scuffle which had taken place between a group of young Communists and five members of the Occupation military police.[23] A letter from General MacArthur to Prime Minister Yoshida, rather than a formal directive, was the means used to purge Japan's Communist party leadership.

---

[21] The Imperial Rule Assistance Association and its affiliates were apparently equated by the Washington and SCAP policy makers with the Nazi Party of Germany. Evaluation of the exact role of the various "Imperial Rule" organizations is not yet available. However, the conclusion is generally accepted that they fell short of monopolizing political power within a monolithic framework. To include them for dissolution under an order (SCAPIN 548) which was primarily concerned with ultranationalistic, secret, and terroristic societies would seem unfair. Yet this is the frame of reference within which they are viewed in the JCS Directive.

[22] SCAPIN 548, paragraphs 1a, 1g. *PRJ*, Vol. II, p. 479.

[23] "Control of Anti-Democratic Elements," p. 33. Typed draft of a proposed supplement to *PRJ* which was to cover the years 1949–1952 and which has not been published.

> Acting in common accord, they [Communist party leaders] have hurled defiance at constituted authority, shown contempt for the processes of law and order, and contrived by false and inflammatory statements and other subversive means to arouse through resulting confusion that degree of social unrest which would set the stage for the eventual overthrow of constitutional government in Japan by force. Their coercive methods bear striking parallel to those by which the militaristic leaders of the past deceived and misled the Japanese people, and their aims, if achieved, would surely lead Japan to an even worse disaster. To permit this incitation to lawlessness to continue unchecked, however embryonic it may at present appear, would be to risk ultimate suppression of Japan's democratic institutions in direct negation of the purpose and intent of Allied policy pronouncements, forfeiture of her chance for political independence, and destruction of the Japanese race. Accordingly, I direct that your government take the necessary administrative measures to remove and exclude the following named persons, constituting the full membership of the Central Committee of the Japan Communist Party, from public service, and render them subject to the prohibitions, restrictions and liabilities of my directives of January 4, 1946 (SCAPIN 548 and 550) and their implementing ordinances. . . .[24]

This letter has been quoted at some length to indicate the kind of reasoning which was used to tie together actions taken under the purge and abolition of societies directives.

The fifth and sixth categories were designed to bring within the scope of the purge semiprivate and public officials who had participated in Japan's program of overseas expansion. Category E dealt with "officers of financial and development organizations" involved in Japan's attempt to create the Greater East Asia Co-Prosperity Spheres. This category represented the sole incursion of the original criteria into the field of economic activity. However, the criteria for purging economic imperialists were far more selective than those which were applied to the military. All career officers were made subject to designation by the purge, but only the top executive group of industrial and financial entrepreneurs was included.[25] Category F dealt with the governmental officials who had ruled the various outposts of the Japa-

[24] General Douglas MacArthur, "Letter to Prime Minister Yoshida," June 6, 1950. This action, so far removed from the purge's original objective of removing militarists and ultranationalists, deserves fuller discussion. Suffice it to say at this point that this step could also be viewed in the light of the situation existing in GHQ in the late spring of 1950. In private conversations, for example, it has been hinted to me that the policy alternatives were between purging the Communist party leadership and outright dissolution of the party. To view this action in such a fashion is to adopt the method of analyzing decisions through the eyes of policy makers. Limitations of this kind of analysis are readily apparent. On occasion, however, they aid in clarifying the context within which a decision is made.

[25] SCAPIN 550, Appendix A, Category E. *PRJ*, Vol. II, p. 485. "Chairman of the Board of Directors, President, Vice-President, Director, and Auditor" of twenty designated concerns.

nese empire during its days of glory. Included in this group were principally governors and certain chief administrators. Again only the very top executive personnel were included in the list of "purgeables."[26] In addition, some of the administrators of the Japanese occupied areas were made subject to the purge since all officials with the civil service rank of *Chokunin* or above, who had served with the War or Navy Ministries, were to be so designated.[27] Most of the areas which fell under Japanese aggression were governed through one or the other of these ministries so that category F was in large part superfluous. Furthermore, the *Chokunin* rank was so high on the bureaucratic ladder that it did not increase the scope of the purge to any considerable extent. In fact, it often hit scholars who had been students of Asian areas then controlled by Japan. They could be persuaded to leave their research and provide the military administrators with expert knowledge and to serve temporarily with the Army or Navy Ministries only by being accorded this, the next to the highest, civil service rank with its attendant perquisites. Often too, these experts were professors at universities who held a civil service rank in the education ministry and could not be hired at a lower rank by the military service ministries.[28]

Category G, the seventh and final one, is the most controversial. Because of its importance, it will be quoted in full.

G. Additional Militarists and Ultranationalists

1. Any person who has denounced or contributed to the seizure of opponents of the militarist regime.

2. Any person who has instigated or perpetrated an act of violence against opponents of the militaristic regime.

3. Any person who has played an active and predominant governmental part in the Japanese program of aggression or who by speech, writing, or action has shown himself to be an active exponent of militant nationalism and aggression.[29]

This category of the purge criteria, designed as a catchall, was the only

[26] SCAPIN 550, Appendix A, Category F. *PRJ*, Vol. II, p. 485. On Formosa, for example, only the positions of governor-general and chief civilian administrator were deemed of sufficient importance; in Malaya, past holders of the post of chief military administrator, chief civilian administrator, and mayor of Singapore were to be subject to designation.

[27] SCAPIN 550, Appendix A, Category B. *PRJ*, Vol. II, p. 484.

[28] Personal knowledge gained while working with government section, SCAP. The hiring of experts, from universities and from the United States federal government departments, who, while serving with the Allied Occupation of Japan, became United States Department of Army or Department of Navy civilians, may be considered analogous. Gaining their services also was often dependent upon high civil service ratings.

[29] SCAPIN 550, Appendix A, Category G. *PRJ*, Vol. II, p. 485.

one in which interpretation of the criteria determined whether or not an individual should be purged. In cases involving criteria under categories A through F, the decision was automatic. For example, either an individual had or had not been a commissioned officer in the regular army. Potentially, therefore, category G endowed great power upon those who were reviewing the careers of Japanese leaders with a view to their eligibility under the purge. Particularly the last clause in paragraph 3 of the category could be used to remove the political opponents of individuals empowered to administer the purge. The Japanese government, however, immediately set about trying to limit the scope of this category by having the cabinet draft detailed interpretations of it.[30] These interpretations again reduced the designation of a purgee[31] to whether he had or had not held a listed position.

The Hatoyama Case

Not in all instances did these more detailed interpretations of category G make the designation of a purgee solely a matter of determining whether an individual had been indicted as a war criminal, had held a commission in the career military services, had been a leader of an ultranationalistic society, had been an officer in one of the Imperial Rule societies, had been an executive in one of the business enterprises which had reaped such a rich harvest from Japan's aggressive expansion, or had been one of the officials charged with administering Japan's empire. On occasion, the administrators of the purge utilized the broad criteria of category G instead of the limiting interpretations worked out by the cabinet.

Hatoyama Ichiro's designation as a purgee in the spring of 1946 was such an instance. If any one case epitomizes the controversies which ebbed and flowed around the purge, it is this *cause célèbre.* Hatoyama had had a distinguished career in Showa[32] politics. He had been chief secretary of the General Tanaka Giichi cabinet from 1927 to 1929. He had been minister of education from 1931 until 1934. He had traveled as personal envoy of Prime Minister Konoye to Europe subsequent to the outbreak of the China "Incident" and had been received by the

[30] *PRJ*, Vol. I, pp. 21–23; 27–28.

[31] There are two meanings of the word "purgee." Either it refers to one who is purgeable under the criteria but has not been designated, or it refers to one who has been designated and removed from public office or excluded from government service. These two meanings merged once the program of provisional designation was instituted under which all persons to whom the purge criteria applied were designated as purgees.

[32] *Showa* (Benevolent Peace) is the era name of the reign of Hirohito which began in 1925.

leaders of Europe, including Hitler and Mussolini. First elected to the House of Representatives in 1915, he was elected in every subsequent general election, including the wartime election of 1942, in which he was returned to his seat in the Diet, although he had not been one of the candidates "recommended" by General Tojo Hideki.[33] His career as a parliamentarian was as long as was his distinguished service to the Seiyukai, one of the two major political parties in pre-World War II Japan. Subsequent to the surrender of Japan, he organized and was elected first president of the Liberal party in November, 1945. In the election of April, 1946, the first following the defeat of Japan, his party won a plurality (142) of seats in the House of Representatives, making Hatoyama the leading contender for the premiership. This was the background of Hatoyama and the political setting when, on the eve of his formal appointment as prime minister, SCAP issued a directive to the imperial Japanese government[34] ordering his removal and exclusion from public office. The reasons for his removal are of sufficient interest to be quoted in full.

a. As Chief Secretary of the Tanaka Cabinet from 1927 to 1929, he necessarily shares responsibility for the formulation and promulgation without Diet approval of amendments to the so-called Peace Preservation Law which made that law the government's chief legal instrument for the suppression of freedom of speech and freedom of assembly, and made possible the denunciation, terrorization, seizure, and imprisonment of tens of thousands of adherents to minority doctrines advocating political, economic, and social reform, thereby preventing the development of effective opposition to the Japanese militaristic regime.

b. As Minister of Education from December 1931 to March 1934, he was responsible for stifling freedom of speech in the schools by means of mass dismissals and arrests of teachers suspected of "leftist" leanings or "dangerous thoughts." The dismissal in May 1933 of Professor Takigawa from the faculty of Kyoto University on Hatoyama's personal order is a flagrant illustration of his contempt for the liberal tradition of academic freedom and gave momentum to the spiritual mobilization of Japan, which under the aegis of the military and economic cliques, led the nation eventually into war.

c. Not only did Hatoyama participate in thus weaving the pattern of ruthless suppression of freedom of speech, freedom of assembly, and freedom of thought, but he also participated in the forced dissolution of farmer-labor bodies. In addition, his indorsement of totalitarianism, specifically in its application to the regimentation and control of labor, is a matter of record. His recommendation that "it would be well" to transplant Hitlerite anti-labor devices to Japan reveals his innate antipathy to the democratic principle of the right of labor freely to organize and to bargain collectively through representatives of its own choice. It is a familiar

[33] Shugiin Jimukyoku, *Shugiin Yoran* (Otsu) (*House of Representatives Handbook*, B), p. 170.

[34] Under the constitution of 1947, the adjective "Imperial" was deleted.

technique of the totalitarian dictatorship, wherever situated, whatever be its formal name, and however be it distinguished, first to weaken and then to suppress the freedom of individuals to organize for mutual benefit. Whatever lip service Hatoyama may have rendered to the cause of parliamentarianism, his sponsorship of the doctrine of regimentation of labor identifies him as a tool of the ultra-nationalistic interests which engineered the reorganization of Japan on a totalitarian economic basis as a pre-requisite to its wars of aggression.

d. By words and deeds he has consistently supported Japan's acts of aggression. In July 1937 he traveled to America and Western Europe as personal emissary of the then Prime Minister Konoye to justify Japan's expansionist program. While abroad he negotiated economic arrangements for supporting the war against China and the subsequent exploitation of that country after subjugation. With duplicity, Hatoyama told the British Prime Minister in 1937 that "China cannot survive unless controlled by Japan," and that the primary motive behind Japan's intervention in China involved the "happiness of the Chinese people."

e. Hatoyama has posed as an anti-militarist. But in a formal address mailed to his constituents during the 1942 election in which he set forth his political credo, Hatoyama referred to the attack on Pearl Harbor as "fortunately . . . a great victory," stated as a fact that the true cause of the Manchuria and China "incidents" was the anti-Japanese sentiment (in China) instigated by England and America, ridiculed those who in 1928 and 1929 had criticized the Tanaka Cabinet, boasted that that cabinet had "liquidated the (previous) weak-kneed diplomacy toward England and America," and gloated that "today the world policy drafted by the Tanaka Cabinet is steadily being realized." This identification of himself with the notorious Tanaka policy of world conquest, whether genuine or merely opportunistic, in and of itself brands Hatoyama as one of those who deceived and misled the people of Japan into militaristic misadventure.[35]

The phraseology supporting Hatoyama's purge illustrates the paradox of the objectives of the purge as a whole, mentioned in the last chapter. From the viewpoint that the purge's objective was to remove those who had deceived and misled the people of Japan to embark on world conquest, the case against Hatoyama leaves much to be desired. It rests on two counts. First, he was an active participant in the government's policy to control dangerous thoughts. Again, he supported General Tanaka's "positive policy" vis-à-vis China. His admiration for Hitler's labor policy is really irrelevant to the purge criteria, though no doubt indicative of his general outlook. This is the crux of the matter. Had the other objective of the purge, that of clearing the decks of Japan's erstwhile leaders so that previously suppressed or younger leaders could come to the fore, been primary, a far more convincing case could have been constructed. Hatoyama, though he had on occasion opposed the military, as in the Saito expulsion from the Diet in

[35] SCAPIN 919, "Removal and Exclusion of Diet Member" May 3, 1946, *PRJ*, Vol. II, pp. 494–495.

1940, had been a leader of the old Japan. Had the purge criteria more effectively reflected the objective of removing this old leadership, Hatoyama would, by far less eloquent verbal gymnastics than are quoted above, clearly have been found ineligible to become prime minister.

Hatoyama's purge also illustrates that a case could be made supporting the purge of almost anyone of consequence on the basis of category G's broad criteria. As noted earlier, these criteria were refined into specific categories by cabinet interpretation and later were used as the basis for extending the purge into the economic and public information media fields.[36] The purge was often criticized as being too rigid and not making allowances for extenuating factors. A choice clearly had to be made at the outset: make the purge categorical and thereby leave little leeway to the administrators, or, set up the criteria in the broadest possible terms and place primary reliance on the discretion of the purgers. The categorical approach had advantages which overrode its rigidities, most important of which was limiting the capriciousness of the purgers. Whatever the justification of Hatoyama's purge, his removal, as well as that of Hirano Rikizo and Matsumoto Jiichiro (to mention only two of several score controversial cases), has been cited by critics to support the thesis that the purge was arbitrary and motivated by political considerations.[37]

One final comment concerning the criteria as originally formulated deserves attention. In emphasis, they were extremely unequal. The whole officer cadre of the Japanese Army and Navy was made subject to the purge, but only the top crust of the bureaucratic and commercial elites was touched. This emphasis on the military reflects common agreement among Occupation administrators that this group was most dangerous to the future peace of the world. Conversely, this emphasis played into the hands of the leaders of Japan who sought to burden the military with responsibility for having deceived and misled the people of Japan.

[36] Cf. chap. iv, pp. 30–40.

[37] Sumimoto Toshio, *Senryo Hiroku*, pp. 54–77.

Chapter IV

THE CRITERIA ARE ENLARGED

The criteria discussed in the last chapter were applied only to individuals holding positions in the national government. Formulators of the purge, from its inception, had considered the necessity of enlarging the scope of the criteria.

> In order to comply fully with the JCS and SWNCC directives it may be necessary to remove and disqualify one further group of Japanese officials from public office, either elective or appointive. This additional group may include other Japanese officials in Japanese ministries and in the prefectural governments who were in policy making positions during the war years and in the years of preparation for the war. By reason of its effect upon the actual operation of government, it was deemed wise to postpone the removal of this category until the effect of the removal required under the order [proposed draft of SCAPIN 550] has been absorbed.[1]

Implementation by stages of relevant parts of the directives of the State, War, Navy, and Joint Chiefs, rather than in one broad sweep, gave tacit consent to counsels of caution. From the very inception of the purge the counselors of caution declared that carrying out this program would result in giving birth to chaos, confusion, and communism.[2] Holders of these views were to be found among GHQ policy makers, influential friends of the old Japan in the United States, and the Japanese themselves (especially among those who were purgees). The essential thesis of this group was clearly formulated in a memorandum to Government Section, at the time when Government Section was considering enlarging the purge to include officials at the local government level and leaders in the business and information media fields. "Nothing must be done to deteriorate this record of the occupation's astonishing tranquility; any move no matter how laudatory under the Potsdam Declaration must be analyzed as to its effects on public peace."[3] Even without documentation to back it up, this thesis played an increasingly vital role in influencing over-all policy.

Local Government Criteria

The basic paradox in the purge criteria became even more apparent by expanding them to include officials at the prefectural, county, city,

[1] Covering memorandum to draft SCAPIN 550 prepared by Government Section, GHQ, SCAP. Quoted in *PRJ*, Vol. I, p. 12.

[2] *PRJ*, Vol. I, p. 8.

[3] "Implementation of the Purge." Memorandum to Government Section from the assistant chief of staff G-2, December 23, 1946.

town, and village levels. Proving that local government officials had played a major role in "deceiving and misleading the Japanese people to embark on world conquest" presented certain difficulties. Extensive consultations took place between occupation authorities and officials of the Japanese government in attempts to formulate criteria governing the local purge. Highlighting some of the basic points at issue in these negotiations are the letters exchanged between the then Premier Yoshida Shigeru and Generals MacArthur and Whitney.

Mr. Yoshida's basic contention was that to expand the purge categories to the local level of government would make subject to the purge persons who had been the objects rather than the enforcers of regimentation. He maintained that this "... regimentation of the military regime had been engineered by a clique of professional soldiers, of government officials, right-wing reactionaries and some members of the zaibatsu...."[4] Rather than argue with this analysis of the forces which controlled Japan during the so-called militarist era, General MacArthur replied in terms of his view of the intent of the Potsdam Declaration: "... The Government's primary purpose underlying the proposed extension of the purge into the sphere of local government is to afford the people the opportunity for new local leadership...."[5] This statement definitely shifts the objective of the purge from removing the (mis)leaders of Japan to creating the conditions for a new leadership to assert itself. However, the criteria necessarily had to be formulated within the framework of the Potsdam Declaration and the subsequent basic policy papers drafted in Washington. SCAP was not an independent agency operating outside of basic policy laid down by Washington or by the multinational agencies which, on paper at least, supervised the Occupation.[6] Only by changing the underlying policy orientation could this shift in objectives inherent in MacArthur's statement have been fully implemented.

---

[4] Prime Minister Yoshida Shigeru, "Letter to General Douglas MacArthur," *PRJ*, Vol. II, pp. 496–497.

[5] General Douglas MacArthur, "Letter to Prime Minister Yoshida Shigeru," November 1, 1946. *PRJ*, Vol. II, p. 498.

[6] For elucidation on this point, cf. W. MacMahon Ball, *Japan: Enemy or Ally?*, pp. 19–42. Ball was British Commonwealth representative on the Allied Commission for Japan. Referral of such a contemplated policy change to the Allied Council for Japan or the Far Eastern Commission for guidance very possibly could have resulted in endlessly prolonging the actual administration of the purge, given the (then incipient) cleavage between the United States and the Soviet Union. Ball notes that when the Soviet delegate, General Kuzma Derevyanko, did ask a question concerning the purge, General Whitney (chief of Government Section) in his reply proceeded to read long lists of dissolved organizations and purgees. This answer was interpreted as indicating that SCAP was doing very well on its own and did not need the advice of the Allied Council.

As a result, extension of the purge criteria to encompass officials in local government had to be accomplished within the strait jacket of criteria applicable at the national level. This meant that the criteria were expanded to include local officials in the ultranationalistic societies, the Imperial Rule societies, and the Imperial Ex-Servicemen's Association. These criteria probably would not have been altered if the objective actually had been the removal of the old leadership in order to pave the way for the new. But, by basing their removal on the oft-quoted paragraph 6 of the Potsdam Declaration, the implication could readily be drawn that the purge of these local officials rested on their participation in the war effort. Yoshida had a point in his criticism of the expansion of the purgeable positions to include local branches of the Imperial Rule Assistance Association. "... There is no doubt that some executive members of central organization should be held responsible for misleading the people to misery and unhappiness but local 'influential members' of the association shared neither 'ideals' nor feeling of comradeship with the central executives. ..."[7]

One way out of this dilemma would have been for MacArthur to make clear (1) that the local level officials of these organizations were not being removed for war guilt, but solely in order to make way for a new leadership; (2) that the position of branch chief of an Imperial Rule society was included in the mandatory purge criteria because it was a readily defined category by means of which it would be possible to draw a distinction between those who were identified with the *ancien régime* and those who were not; (3) that in short, the purge was a handy tool whereby to clear the decks of the old leadership since the prefectural governor or the city mayor or the village headman had been the local branch chief of the Imperial Rule Assistance Association. Without this distinction, amorphous as it might appear to be, Yoshida could maintain that "The purge should be carried out with thorough conviction of the people 'that justice is being done where it is due' and

[7] Yoshida Shigeru, "Letter," October 31, 1946. *PRJ*, Vol. II, pp. 496–497. Yoshida in the latter part of the letter, comments "With regard to 'influential members of the Imperial Rule Assistance Association' it seems to me that the 'definition' for the 'influential members' was decided by the original interpretation of your Purge Directive but in view of the opinion of the Government Section of GHQ, SCAP, the Japanese government proposed to exclude those chiefs of cities, towns, and villages who happened to be the local chiefs of the Imperial Rule Assistance Association, ex officio, although I am still of the opinion that the part they played in dragging the country to war is almost nil, if any. But to include other local 'influential members' which actually means small functionaries, under the Purge is not only unreasonable but also unjust." ("Influential members" of local branches were not included in the final purge criteria. Cabinet and Home Affairs Ministry Ordinance No. 1, January 4, 1947, Appendix I, Paragraph IV. *PRJ*, Vol. II, p. 513).

when it goes beyond the limit, it is bound to cause distrust of the Government and the purge."[8]

One compromise between the use of the purge as a method whereby new leaders could come to the fore and the war guilt frame of reference of the criteria was that certain mayors and village headmen could not succeed themselves in office. With the advent of the new constitution in May, 1947, these offices would become elective. In order to insure that these local officials would not be able to perpetuate themselves in office, and to accomplish this without invoking the purge, a separate ordinance was promulgated.[9] In brief, this law provided that although not subject to the purge, certain specified local officials[10] who had held office from or before September 1, 1945, to September 1, 1946, should be barred from their posts for a period of four years from the date of the first election subsequently held. Since the purge criteria, because of the Potsdam Declaration framework, could list in the mandatory purge categories only positions held before the ending of the war, these immediate postwar appointments could readily escape removal. This particular law is the sole example in which the problem of the continuity of old leadership is faced squarely without reference to the purge. There is in this approach the germ of a real answer to the problem of how to create conditions whereby a new leadership could come to the fore. Had it been used on a larger scale, the results that the purge achieved might have been significantly altered. However, the Potsdam Declaration's frame of reference precluded this being done.

Certain other problems were faced in formulating the purge criteria affecting local government officials. Curiously enough, it was extremely difficult to convince the Japanese government of the importance of barring from positions in the national government persons purged from provincial posts. Japanese opposition to this provision was based on the fact that certain officials who had already moved from prefectural posts to positions in the national government would be affected. Yoshida summarized these arguments by writing:

> ... It has now been instructed by Government Section that this discrimination between national and local public office holders should not exist and, any one barred from local "public office" should also be barred from all other "public offices," i.e., including "public office" at the national governmental level. Supposing the instruc-

[8] Yoshida Shigeru, *loc. cit.*

[9] Imperial Ordinance No. 3, January 4, 1947. *PRJ*, Vol. II, p. 507.

[10] Mayors and deputy mayors of cities, headmen and deputy headmen of towns and villages, ward headmen in Tokyo metropolis and persons holding corresponding positions thereto. Imperial Ordinance No. 3, Article II. *PRJ*, Vol. II, p. 507.

tion were taken into effect, it would mean excluding or removing quite a number of the present members of the Diet who held some local "public office" at one time. I think the consequence would be most serious because the very question of faith and integrity of the Government would be involved.[11]

In effect, Yoshida was pleading to permit persons purged from local government posts to remain in or move into positions in the national government. As a compromise, the application of the enlarged purge criteria which included local governmental posts was delayed until the screening of candidates for the general election of April, 1947.

A brief reference to the political situation is necessary to indicate the reasoning that lay behind Premier Yoshida's questionable view that a person designated as a purgee for having held a post in one of the provincial branches of the Imperial Rule societies, for example, should not be barred from greater responsibility at the national level. On its face, the proposal has a bizarre quality. We must take into consideration the fact that the dominant postwar conservative parties, subsequent to the removal of some of their national political leaders on the basis of the initial purge criteria, had relied on local party men to fill the void.[12] Many of these replacements had been influential in local politics and were thus well known to the local electorate. Their presence in the Diet certainly aided Premier Yoshida during the spring of 1947, when a revision of the election law was passed that would benefit the conservative parties.[13] Had they been removed from national office when the new criteria were officially promulgated in January, the electoral revision that was pushed through in March might not have become the law governing that election. Furthermore, their disqualification at an early date could not but impress the grass-roots electorates that leaders of the old regime, regardless of whether they had been important in national or in provincial politics, were undesirable in the eyes of the Occupation. Taken in conjunction, these factors might have appreciably altered the results of the April, 1947, election which came during the high tide of the reformist era.

In opposition to the removal of these individuals who were potential purgees under the enlarged criteria, Yoshida pointed out that, "... Based on your Purge Directive, the Government officially approved of their 'qualifications' one day and still basing decisions on the same directive, the Government could not, on another day, disapprove of

[11] Yoshida Shigeru, *loc. cit.*
[12] Kenneth E. Colten, "Prewar Influence in Post-War Conservative Parties," pp. 940–956.
[13] T. A. Bisson, *Prospects for Democracy in Japan,* pp. 56–58.

their qualifications. . . ."[14] Premier Yoshida quite correctly could assert that to clear individuals on the basis of an Occupation directive and then to reverse the decision at a later date, while retaining the basis for that taken earlier, would raise serious questions concerning his "faith and integrity."[15] It is implicit in this statement that if General MacArthur wanted to change the ground rules of the purge, he, and not Premier Yoshida, should bear the onus of responsibility. In effect, the prime minister was asking for a new directive. Issuance of this, however, would run counter to the MacArthur " . . . policy of encouraging the Japanese Government through informal discussion to take the initiative in this type of problem. . . ."[16] Reversal of this policy would undermine the validity of the press releases emanating from SCAP that the Japanese people were reforming themselves. Caught within the mesh of his own propaganda, therefore, General MacArthur could not press the Japanese government too severely in expanding the criteria in a manner consistent with the basic objectives of the purge. Small wonder that the resultant criteria were a bundle of compromises and contradictions.

Formulating the Economic Purge Criteria

The controversial nature of the purge program as a whole pales considerably in comparison to that generated by proposals to expand the purge into spheres of economic activity. In large part, because of its controversial character, expansion of the purge into this sphere was not as complete as the initial postsurrender policies directed, and it bogged down on two counts. First, its implementation was delayed; its timing was thus comparable to that of expanding the criteria to local government levels. Moreover, as a result of the length of time devoted to them, the criteria became models of obscurity and complexity.

The Joint Chiefs had been no less clear-cut in their orders concerning leaders in the economic sphere of activity than they had been concerning important political and military personnel.

> You will prohibit the retention in or selection for positions of important responsibility or influence in industry, finance, commerce, or agriculture of all persons who have been active exponents of militant nationalism and aggression. . . . In the absence of evidence, satisfactory to you, to the contrary, you will assume that any persons who have held key positions of high responsibility since 1937, in industry, finance, commerce, or agriculture have been *active exponents of militant nationalism and aggression.*[17]

---

[14] Yoshida Shigeru, *loc. cit.*
[15] *Ibid.*
[16] *PRJ*, Vol. I, p. 31.
[17] JCS Directive (paragraph 23), *PRJ*, Vol. II, p. 435. (Italics mine.)

The same paragraph also noted that all those "who do not direct future Japanese effort solely towards peaceful ends"[18] should not be retained. Policies designed to guide the redevelopment of the Japanese economy, however, were couched in terms of encouraging "a wide distribution of income and ownership of the means of production" which were to be "organized on a democratic basis."[19] Bifurcation of objectives is again to be noted. Economic leaders were to be judged on their participation in the war effort and their willingness to pursue their tasks toward peaceful ends. Economic organizations, however, were to become democratic.

The economic purge, as this part of the program came to be known in SCAP jargon, had a partial beginning in the initial formulation of the criteria. Some of the leaders of certain corporations which had engaged in overseas economic expansionist activities had been included.[20] Full implementation of the Joint Chiefs' directive quoted above was delayed for well over one year. The official history of the purge program in explaining this decision to delay implementation relates the following:

> The implementation of those portions of the JCS directive dealing with the economic fields was left for a later date, first, because extensive research and study were deemed necessary to prepare adequate criteria, and second, to insure that the program would cause a minimum of disruption to the necessary effort toward economic recovery.[21]

Adequate study and research take time. To delay application of the purge until this research and study were accomplished could contribute to better achievement of desired results. This kind of reasoning, however, also could be applied to the formulation of all the purge criteria. Similar study had been required and accomplished during the early months of the occupation to arrive at the purge criteria in other fields. Why then was it not done with regard to positions in spheres of economic activity? Many factors played a role. One was that Economic and Scientific Section[22] had been unable to receive approval for its draft outlining the criteria for the economic purge.[23] A second factor resulted from this, namely, that there was debate on the advisability of removing captains of industry. In part, the position taken by the adversaries depended upon their analysis of the extent to which the leaders of the

---

[18] *Ibid.*

[19] JCS Directive (paragraph 25), *PRJ*, Vol. II, p. 435.

[20] SCAPIN 550, Appendix A, Category E. *PRJ*, Vol. II, p. 485.

[21] *PRJ*, Vol. I, p. 46.

[22] One of the special staff sections in GHQ, SCAP.

[23] T. A. Bisson, *Zaibatsu Dissolution in Japan*, p. 160. Mr. Bisson notes, "The full history of the [1946] summer's debate [within GHQ] on this issue, a long and interesting one, lies buried in GHQ files."

Japanese economy had been, as the Joint Chiefs phrased it, "active exponents of militant aggression." In short, the basic reason for needing extensive research and study was a lack of desire by the policy making officials in the Occupation, not to mention those in the Japanese government, to tamper with Japan's economic base.

The second reason given for delaying the economic purge is more specious. Justifying the procrastination by alluding to the desire not to hamper Japan's economic recovery made some sense in the spring of 1948.[24] By then, it could be maintained that international considerations were of such overweening importance that any efforts toward domestic reform were useless. However, to make it seem as if these same international considerations played an important role in delaying the implementation of the economic purge is misleading. As late as January, 1947, General MacArthur stated, "In my opinion, and I believe in the opinion of truly responsible Japanese as well, the action of extending the purge into industrial and financial circles will not unduly disturb the development of a future peaceful industrial economy."[25]

The timing of the implementation of the economic purge was important in influencing the degree to which a new leadership could be given an opportunity to emerge in the Japanese economy. Occupation policy had begun its shift of emphasis from reform to recovery by the time the economic purge began in the spring of 1947. The crucial factor in this change of emphasis was the gradual acceptance by policy makers that recovery would be aided by discarding reform. Furthermore, nearly eighteen months had passed since the initial formulation of the purge criteria. This was ample time for the purgeable captains of industry and finance to put into key positions trusted lieutenants who would continue to take orders from them. This continuation of influence might have taken place no matter how soon the economic purge had been applied. However, if the removals could have been made in all spheres of activity at the same time, the relative impact on entrenched leadership might have been appreciably greater. A new leadership, with an outlook more in consonance with those ideals which the Joint Chiefs directed SCAP to encourage, might have faced fewer obstacles in its development.[26]

---

[24] At which time the official history was being prepared.

[25] General MacArthur's comment on a *Newsweek* article entitled, "Behind the Japanese Purge—American Military Rivalries." *PRJ*, Vol. II, p. 549.

[26] No lessening of obstacles would by themselves assure that the new leadership would have an outlook different from that which had been removed. The reader is asked to remember that the purge was only one small part of the over-all Occupation effort to redirect Japanese society.

Innumerable drafts, proposals, and counter-proposals by interested staff sections in GHQ and the Japanese government constituted the research and study which took so much time. Only by so doing, however, could Government Section obtain sufficient statistical data "to gauge accurately the nature and extent of the program which must be instituted."[27] Finally, to prod the Japanese government into action, SCAPIN 548, the purge directive's companion calling for the dissolution of certain types of organizations, was employed as a tool. Criteria setting forth bases for deciding whether an association should be dissolved included the following:

1. Support or justification of aggressive Japanese military action abroad, or

2. Exclusion of foreign persons in Japan from trade, commerce, or the exercise of their profession.[28]

Full application of its terms to economic organizations would have meant complete liquidation and removal of managerial personnel down to and including influential members of the staff. Had such action been taken, it would have approximated more closely the initial post-surrender policy for the disposition of Japan's economic masters. As in the case of the officers of the Imperial Rule societies and in the later removal of the Japan Communist party's leadership, a compromise was effectuated. Under its terms, only selected officials in certain specifically designated concerns were made subject to the purge.[29]

The length of time taken in their formulation was matched by the complexity of the criteria on the basis of which the economic purge was implemented. Within the original purge criteria, the economic purge was incorporated as a new category under the catchall G clause, "additional militarists and ultranationalists."[30] This was to cover important officers in the following types of concerns:

---

[27] *PRJ*, Vol. I, p. 47.

[28] SCAPIN 548, Articles 1b and 1d, *PRJ*, Vol. II, p. 479.

[29] By utilizing SCAPIN 548, Government Section accomplished two objectives. First, it galvanized the Japanese government into action. Three months elapsed between calling for a Japanese government plan which would be used as the basis for the economic purge criteria and its submission to GHQ. This delay, coming as it did after months of collaboration between the Japanese government and Economic and Scientific Section on a workable economic purge, indicates the probability that the Japanese government had not given serious consideration to the economic purge until substantially more rigid action had been suggested. Second, Government Section, instead of Economic and Scientific Section, won jurisdiction over the implementation of the economic purge since it was Government Section which had jurisdiction over the implementation of SCAPIN 548. Which section would have jurisdiction was of importance in that Economic and Scientific Section had been unable to receive approval within GHQ for its version of the economic purge and had subsequently indicated unwillingness to do anything further about it.

[30] SCAPIN 550, Appendix A, category G. *PRJ*, Vol. II, p. 485.

a. Conspicuously influential companies which have manufactured finished aircraft or arms, or munitions, or strategic or critical materials essential to the construction thereof.

b. Conspicuously monopolistic companies which have engaged in production of basic productive materials or business of communication or transportation.

c. Conspicuously monopolistic companies which have engaged in domestic or foreign trade.

d. Holding companies designated or to be designated hereafter by SCAP memoranda and influential companies closely associated with the above.[31]

e. Companies which have authorized capitalization exceeding one hundred million yen.

f. Any other companies or financial institutions which have commanded excessive economic power.[32]

A gap can be readily noted between the objective of removing militarists and ultranationalists and the above criteria. "Conspicuously monopolistic companies" or companies "commanding excessive economic power" are not phrases that readily bring to mind warlike activities. On the other hand, these criteria do make sense if emphasis is given to the objective of establishing an economy in which income and ownership are to be widely distributed.[33] Had the criteria been tied more closely to the program dissolving Japan's monopoly combines, they would have had more meaning.[34]

Rather than let the agencies charged with administering the purge determine the industrial and financial enterprises which fell within the scope of these criteria, long lists set them forth. Listed companies, in which holders of important positions during the critical period were automatically subject to the purge, numbered two hundred and forty-five, of which, however, only one hundred and fifty-one were still operative in Japan.[35] The critical period was defined as being from July 7, 1937,[36] to September 2, 1945. Key positions in these corporations included the following:

---

[31] This provision was modified in January, 1949, at the request of Economic and Scientific Section to include not all of the companies so designated. No explanation for this change is known. However, the action is indicative of the watering down of the economic purge criteria. *PRJ*, Vol. I, p. 52.

[32] Cabinet and Home Ministry Ordinance No. 1 of 1947, Appendix I, paragraph VII, "Remarks," paragraph 6–(1), (2), (3), (4), (5), (6). *PRJ*, Vol. II, p. 526.

[33] JCS Directive, paragraph 25 a, b. *PRJ*, Vol. II, p. 435.

[34] For elucidation on this point, cf. T. A. Bisson, *Zaibatsu Dissolution in Japan*, pp. 175–179.

[35] *Ibid.*, p. 163.

[36] Outbreak of the China "Incident."

Chairman (Kai cho)
Vice-chairman (Fuku-Kaicho)
President (Shacho)
Vice-President (Fuku-Shacho)
Managing Director (Senmu Torishimari Yaku)
Standing Director (Jomu Torishimari Yaku)
Standing Auditor (Jonin Kansa Yaku)
Active Advisor (Komon) or
Councilor (Sodan Yaku)
Principal stockholder who owned 10 per cent or more of the capital stocks or who exercised, directly or indirectly, controlling influence in the management of the company, or any other official, regardless of his title, including branch managers in Japanese occupied territory, Axis or Axis-occupied country, who in fact exercised authority or influence commensurate with that of any of the positions listed above. . . .[37]

These criteria have been quoted in full to illustrate the lengths to which they were spelled out. Because of their explicit directions, changes in them could be made only with the greatest difficulty. Such changes as were made were deletions rather than additions.[38]

Addition of further categories of economic institutions whose managerial personnel were classified as holding "public office" made the final criteria even more involved. In turn, positions classified as "public office" were divided into "principal" and "ordinary" public office.[39] This distinction was of considerable importance, since an individual, even though designated as a purgee, could continue to hold "ordinary" public office. He was, however, barred from "principal" public office.[40] A purgee, if he were satisfied with a position defined as ordinary public office, could continue to exercise his influence by means of this distinction. If research and study can produce such models of complexity as these criteria, we can be thankful that all the purge criteria were not so lengthily analyzed. Much time was devoted to the formulation of this exercise in obscurantism. In turn, this affected the timing of the economic purge. A larger issue is thereby raised.

[37] Cabinet and Home Ministry Ordinance No. 1 of 1947, paragraph VII, "Remarks," paragraph 6. *PRJ*, Vol. I, pp. 51–52. (The 10 per cent stockholder provision was not applied. Cf. *PRJ*, Vol. I, p. 52.)

[38] *PRJ*, Vol. I, pp. 51–52.

[39] Cabinet Home Ministry Ordinance No. 1 of 1947, Appendix II, paragraphs 6-12. *PRJ*, Vol. II, pp. 529–543. To add another element of confusion, specified key officials in companies listed under paragraph 11 who had served during the critical period, i.e., between 1937 and 1945, were automatically subject to the purge. Paragraphs 6 through 10 and paragraph 12 served solely to list organizations, leading positions in which were defined as being within public service.

[40] Imperial Ordinance No. 1 of 1947, Article III: "Any person who falls under the provisions of Appendix 'A' to the Memorandum, i.e., the purge criteria, in case he holds any ordinary public office, may be removed therefrom." *PRJ*, Vol. II, p. 501.

The most frequent criticism of the economic purge is that it deprived Japan of its most capable managerial talent. Individuals described as having been and being "friendliest to the United States . . . and who had and would in the future contribute to the basis of capitalism and free enterprise in Japan" were affected as a class.[41] Further, it was contended that their absence retarded Japan's economic recovery. Yet rehabilitation of the Japanese economy did not seriously begin until the end of 1947, by which time the surface influence of this managerial talent had been removed. Hence, economic development took place at a time when this leadership was not available.[42] Neither critic nor supporter of the purge has ever taken the position that it did not remove some very able men. One of its primary objectives had been to do so. So long as this talent had to be removed—that is, so long as the Occupation adhered to its international policy commitments—Japan's recovery would probably have been aided if the removals had been swift and accomplished in one sweep. Economic recovery was retarded by valuable time spent in formulating the criteria with utmost care, not so much because leadership was lacking, but rather because available talent was uncertain of its future. Had the purge been implemented rapidly, the full energies of the Occupation, the Japanese government, and the Japanese people could have been turned toward rehabilitation. Furthermore, rehabilitation would have been accomplished by a leadership different from that which had geared Japan's economy for war.

Formulating Public Information Media Criteria

Japanese personnel in certain large newspaper institutions provided the original impetus for bringing purge criteria to bear upon public information enterprises. In the fall of 1945, the newly created unions of Japan's three largest newspapers[43] forced the resignation of the top officials. They were charged with having advocated militarism and ultranationalism.[44] Civil Information and Education Section, the special staff section in GHQ charged with supervising developments in information media, had made an early effort in the spring of 1946 to aid in the

[41] Harry J. Kern, "Trouble in Japan," p. 24.

[42] Many factors, other than the availability or nonavailability of talented leadership, played a role in Japan's economic rehabilitation.

[43] The *Asahi*, *Mainichi*, and *Yomiuri* newspapers.

[44] Miriam S. Farley, *Aspects of Japan's Labor Problems*, p. 101. In the official history, the role played by the unions in these developments was given only one reference which was couched in the euphemism "guild" instead of "union." The purge had been attacked in so many quarters as being "communist" or "leftist" inspired, that to admit one phase of the purge had been foreshadowed by eighteen months of labor union activity, was apparently considered as adding fuel to these charges, and hence was deliberately soft-pedaled. Cf. *PRJ*, Vol. I, p. 58.

process of leadership change by drafting a directive with this objective in mind.[45] As in the economic purge, this effort remained abortive until commensurate criteria were brought within the framework of the political purge as implemented by Government Section.

GHQ was uncertain about the position it should take in response to the efforts of Japanese newspaper unions to remove ultranationalists and militarists from managerial posts. This uncertainty of the Occupation was important in delaying application of the purge in this field. The union-sponsored management had instituted editorial policies which were not only critical of Japan's old regime but also began to voice veiled criticisms of the dilatory approach by the Occupation to basic reforms. As a result, the old, presumably discredited leadership was given relatively free rein by Occupation authorities in reinstating itself in power.[46] It is further ironical that the union-sponsored management had initially antagonized Occupation authorities by criticizing reform policies announced by SCAP. Had the Occupation taken advantage of these early spontaneous developments by immediately drawing up a program which would aid this new leadership, a tremendous stimulus to unfettered thought would have been provided. Instead, the public information media criteria were the last to be implemented.

A problem in legal interpretation faced the SCAP personnel. Neither SWNCC nor the JCS directive had included public information media as a field from which undesirable leadership was to be removed. The question of whether or not the press and publishing lords, moviemakers, theater producers, writers, artists, and scholars had played a role in deceiving and misleading the people of Japan to embark on world conquest was more basic to the issue.[47] Action taken by Japanese labor leaders in newspapers (and subsequently in the motion-picture industry) would point to an affirmative answer by those best informed and thus best equipped to give this kind of judgment. In the final analysis, even the legal issue was settled by the Occupation's adoption, albeit after some delay, of a policy endorsing this viewpoint.

The criteria for the public information media purge were even more complex than those for the economic purge. In part, their complexity was the result of protracted studies of the field which necessitated two

---

[45] *PRJ*, Vol. I, p. 59.

[46] Robert H. Berkov, "The Press in Postwar Japan," p. 164. Cf. also William J. Coughlin, *Conquered Press*, p. 72. "The sweeping from office of the reactionaries who ran the press was indeed most desirable, but the manner in which it was carried out by the newspaper unions placed some newspapers in the hands of equally irresponsible elements and later *forced SCAP to take firm action to place control of the press in proper hands.*" (Italics mine.)

[47] Paraphrase of Article 6 of the Potsdam Declaration, *PRJ*, Vol. II, p. 413.

special subcommittees being established for this purpose;[48] also, in part, the lengths to which the criteria needed to be refined was the result of the far-flung character of the information field. As finally evolved, the criteria covered activities of the following categories of groups and individuals: (1) government officials who had participated in propaganda and guidance of thought and speech toward jingoistic ends, (2) members of the Diet who had been conspicuously active in support of jingoism as evidenced by speeches and writings, (3) scholars, journalists, or publicists who had beaten the drum of aggression, and (4) important officials in newspaper companies and news agencies, book- and magazine-publishing houses, motion-picture and theatrical production companies, and in the broadcasting corporation, whose activities provided evidence of having been militarists or ultranationalists.[49]

All criteria were spelled out in minute detail. For government officials, there were included only top-flight policy posts in the Home, Education, Communications, and Justice ministries as well as certain high-ranking offices in the Metropolitan Police Board, the Board of Information, and the Planning Board of the cabinet. For them the critical period of service was from 1937 to 1945. For important officials in information media enterprises, the categories of activity proscribed ex post facto by SCAPIN 548[50] were used as evidence that the corporations which these officials controlled had contributed to the development of a militaristic and ultranationalistic temperament among the people. For them the critical period of service was defined as being from July, 1937, to December, 1941 (rather than until the end of World War II in 1945) because subsequent to the attack on Pearl Harbor, the government had exercised such stringent controls that deviationist commentary had not been permitted. The task of determining which information companies had contributed to ultranationalistic, jingoistic, and chauvinistic thought fell to the special information subcommittees. Two considerations guided their selection. The first was the company's influence as determined by magazine or newspaper circulation figures, number of books printed, or number of movies and theatrical

[48] *PRJ*, Vol. I, p. 62. The first, composed largely of government officials, proved itself incapable of fulfilling its mandate. The second, composed of the Director of the Imperial Library Okada Naro; three professors of literature, Odaka Kunio, Ota Ryoichi and Kaneko Takezo; a professor of economics, Kameshima Taiji; and a professor of political science, Hori Toyoo, systematically reviewed all Japanese publications during the period critical for the information purge, i.e., July, 1937 to December, 1941.

[49] Cabinet and Home Ministry Ordinance No. 1 of 1947, Appendix I, paragraph VII, "Remarks," paragraphs 5a, b, c, d. *PRJ*, Vol. II, pp. 517–525.

[50] SCAPIN 548, "Abolition of Certain Political Parties, Associations, Societies, and Other Organizations," paragraph 1a–g. *PRJ*, Vol. II, p. 479.

productions offered. The second was the frequency with which the company's efforts had been concerned with propaganda activities.[51] For example, the *Japan Times and Mail,* considered to have been the official organ of the Japanese Foreign Office, was not included on the proscribed list. In spite of its substantial influence, reasoned the subcommittee, it had been published in English and consequently its circulation was small in comparison to the Japanese language newspapers.[52] Concomitant with this work, the subcommittee studied the managerial structure in each organization to determine which positions should be defined as having been of controlling influence in matters of policy.

For reviewing the careers of publicists, the information media subcommittees formulated yet another set of criteria. These are of sufficient interest to be quoted in full.

> 1. Advocated aggression or militant nationalism, or actively contributed to such propaganda, or who through his political or philosophical doctrine laid down an ideological basis for the policies for the Greater East Asia, New Order in the Far East, or policies of similar nature, or the Manchurian Incident, or the Pacific War.
> 2. Advocated dictatorship or totalitarianism of the Nazi or Fascist pattern.
> 3. Advocated the supremacy of the Japanese nation to be a leader of other nations or who coöperated actively with propaganda of the above effect.
> 4. Persecuted or denounced liberals or persons espousing anti-militaristic ideologies.
> 5. In any other way advocated or championed militarism or ultrationalism.[53]

History moves quickly. These criteria were formulated in 1947. Only a short time later many responsible officials in the United States, as well as in Japan, expressed the belief that it was Japan's duty to assume some of these obligations of leadership (especially no. 3) in eastern Asia. These criteria, though broad and all-inclusive at face value, were interpreted strictly so that only a small number (286) of scholars and writers were designated.[54]

Incursion by the purge into the information media field presented its enforcers with delicate issues. Most serious was the possibility that a new form of thought control could be introduced. To be sure, it would be control after the fact and not before. Also, the speed of history al-

[51] *PRJ*, Vol. I, p. 63.

[52] For another aspect of this case, cf. chap. vii, pp. 95–97.

[53] Cabinet and Home Affairs Ministry Ordinance No. 1 of 1947, Appendix I, paragraph VII, "Remarks," paragraphs 5c (1), (2), (3), (4), (5). *PRJ*, Vol. II, pp. 518–519.

[54] Three hundred thirty-one were initially designated as purgees of whom 45 presented acceptable counterevidence to the screening committee. "Statistical Summary of Purge," *PRJ*, Vol. II, p. 564.

most precluded the formulation of criteria proscribing certain policy orientations. Under these circumstances, any move to restrict expressions of thought runs the risk of being outdated before its proponents have been silenced. The charge that the information media purge was stringent is thus hardly substantiated. In fact, quite the reverse is believed to have been true. If the formulators erred, it was on the side of leniency.

Summary

The basic orientation of the purge criteria shifted markedly in the course of its expansion. The Occupation attempted to make the criteria conform more closely to the broader objective of the democratization of Japan, rather than to continue formulating criteria on the basis of war guilt. This significant switch is particularly noticeable in Occupation rationalizations concerning the criteria affecting local government officials and leaders of private economic enterprises. Ultimate justification, however, remained couched in the war guilt terms of reference. The reasons for this are twofold. First, the Occupation would have had to face the issue of who was actually prodemocratic or antidemocratic in the Japanese setting. This issue need not be faced so long as the criteria could be justified as removing those who had deceived and misled the people of Japan. Second, a basic policy decision at the international control level would have been needed to reorient the purge in this manner. Contradictory definitions of democracy from the nations represented on the Far Eastern Commission and the Allied Council of Japan made it impossible to arrive at an acceptable substitute for the war guilt formula of the Potsdam Declaration and initial postsurrender policy documents. Hence, though the orientation of the purge at the enforcement level was altered, justification of the criteria on the basis of war guilt remained necessary. By continuing to use evidence of chauvinism and jingoism to justify the addition of certain criteria, critics of the purge had a field day in being able to point out numerous contradictions. Outraged cries at the injustice of it all were often legitimate, given the war guilt terms of reference, since many of those affected could often provide evidence of having participated in the war effort only to the extent that they had fulfilled the minimal obligations of patriotism. This criticism would have fallen by the wayside if the criteria had been frankly, instead of surreptitiously, justified on the basis of being a tool by means of which the old leadership could be discarded.

A quantitative pattern emerges in analyzing the purge criteria as a whole. The initial criteria were sweeping in form, for example, for career military service officers *in toto;* but they were limited in scope, applying only to positions in the national government. The expanded criteria were more inclusive in that they encompassed local government, private industry, and media of public information; but because of their complex and detailed character were considerably more limited in form. Designating an individual as a purgee gradually became a cut and dried process, for the only determinant was his fulfillment or nonfulfillment of any of the detailed criteria. Since the purge was carried out by administrative proceedings, this development was propably both necessary and inevitable. However, it became more difficult to remove a person who, though clearly undesirable from the viewpoint of furthering the democratization process, did not fall within any of the established purge criteria. By the same token, very little leeway could be provided in granting exemptions.

In conclusion, the timing of the whole purge program was thrown out of kilter by delaying the formulation of the purge criteria for local government, business enterprises, and information media personnel. This procrastination was defended on the basis that it would aid in continuing the tranquillity of the Occupation. Whatever one's position on this issue, the deleterious effects of the decision to delay were substantial. A period of nearly eighteen months was available to those eventually removed, in which time they were able to exercise their authority and to train their subordinates to continue their policies. In the information media purge, the Occupation missed a real opportunity to aid a spontaneous program directed toward the same ends as those envisaged by the purge. Finally, by the time the enlarged purge criteria were applied, the initial reformist *élan* had dissipated itself, and the Occupation had moved to a position of sponsoring recovery. In turn this meant that the old leadership, far from being any longer discredited, was frequently welcomed by the Occupation to help rebuild Japan along traditionalist lines.

CHAPTER V

PROBLEMS OF ADMINISTRATION

BASIC POLICY and purge criteria delineated the scope of the program to effectuate a change in the composition and policy orientation of Japan's leadership. Its effectiveness, however, was also influenced considerably by the administrative mechanism which implemented its terms. Because of the public relations consciousness of General MacArthur, observers of the Occupation often received the impression that, with the issuance of a directive from SCAP to the Japanese government, or the latter's promulgation of a law complying therewith, that which had been only directed had been already accomplished. "The Public Relations Section of SCAP seemed to place little confidence in the art of understatement."[1] It is not surprising, then, that often a basic reform directive or a subsequent Japanese government ordinance was carefully worked out, but the administrative implementation was haphazard. Certainly this was true in the purge program.

The problems of administration altered as the purge passed through its several phases of formulating the criteria, screening holders of and applicants for public office, provisionally designating all potential purgees and supervising their activities, and handling appeals to remove designation. Diffusion of responsibility was a constant problem at several levels. Initially, there was a diffusion of responsibility within General Headquarters, both at the policy and at the operating levels. Subsequently, although the Japanese government bore responsibility officially, in reality it was Government Section which had supervisory and review powers, thus being responsible for action in a number of crucial cases. Finally, responsibility in Japanese government administration was divided at the central governmental level between a screening committee and an appeals board.

ADMINISTRATIVE VS. JUDICIAL PROCEEDINGS

A second major problem concerning the implementation of the purge is of a more general nature. The categorical approach was effectuated by means of administrative procedures, and recourse to the judiciary was undertaken only for violations of the purge ordinances.[2] Before

[1] W. MacMahon Ball, *Japan: Enemy or Ally*, p. 19.

[2] These injunctions included, e.g., omitting relevant data from the questionnaire, or engaging in political activities. They will be discussed more fully below, pp. 69–76.

the administrative machinery began to function, the Japanese government suggested another alternative. Instead of using the categorical approach, it was suggested that a commission should be charged with determining "upon *prima facie* evidence whether the careers and activities of the persons in question deserve their removal and exclusion from office. . . ."[3] Clarity of expression is lacking in this statement, but the suggestion implies that the commission should investigate all aspects of an individual's background in order to arrive at a decision concerning his fitness to serve in the new Japan. As such, its intent was in basic disagreement with the terms of the directive which ordered the removal and exclusion of all those who had held proscribed positions as defined in Appendix A to SCAPIN 550.[4] Had the Japanese proposal been accepted it would have changed the designation process from administrative to judicial. In replying to his suggestion, General Whitney relied on the intent of the purge.

> The purpose of the Directive is to cleanse the Japanese government of elements which by their *acts* or *associations* participated in Japanese expansion. The directive is not *punitive* (as the Japanese proposal implied) but, on the contrary, it is preventive. It is a necessary precaution against the resurgence of Japanese expansionist tendencies; therefore, until after the directive has been complied with, individual "guilt" (which requires inquiry into *intent* as distinguished from *act*) is irrelevant.[5]

Premier Shidehara's proposal to temper the categorical approach by reviewing an individual's entire career had much to commend it. Each applicant for or holder of a public office would be judged not only on his having held a particular office, but also on his active support of the government's warlike and aggressive policies. Furthermore, as General Whitney notes, the individual's intent while holding office would

---

[3] "Informal confidential memorandum" from the Japanese government to Chief, Government Section, SCAP. January, 1946. Quoted in *PRJ*, Vol. I, p. 17.

[4] Paragraph 2, SCAPIN 550. *PRJ*, Vol. II, p. 482. "The Imperial Japanese Government is hereby ordered to remove from public office and exclude from government service all persons who have been: (a) active exponents of militaristic nationalism and aggression; (b) influential members of any Japanese ultranationalistic, terroristic, or secret patriotic society, its agencies or affiliates; or (c) influential in the activities of the Imperial Rule Assistance Association, the Imperial Rule Assistance Political Society, or the Political Association of Great Japan, as those terms are defined in Appendix 'A' to this Directive." Paragraph 5, SCAPIN 550, "An official removed under this procedure will be summarily dismissed and will not be entitled to the hearing or other procedures precedent to his removal to which he may have been entitled under Japanese law."

[5] Interview with Shidehara; "Memorandum from Chief, Government Section to SCAP," January 25, 1946, as quoted in *PRJ*, Vol. I, p. 18.

affect the disposition of his case by the commission of inquiry.[6] An attempt to cast the purge into the mold of the war crimes trials is implicit in the Japanese government's approach to this issue. To the Japanese, the central issue is that of responsibility for Japan's militantly aggressive policies. Possibly a removal program based on these premises would have been fairer or would have conformed more closely to the ideals of justice. However, an initial choice had to be made between giving discretion to the purgers and making the purge criteria specific and final. Once the decision in favor of defining the purge criteria on the basis of definite positions had been made, the best the Japanese government could hope to accomplish was to restrict them as narrowly as possible.[7] To expect judicial interpretation of the criteria as they affected individuals was to expect too much.

Utilization of the Japanese government's approach to the designation process would have posed certain difficulties. It would have slowed up immeasurably the determination of who was and who was not a purgee. Despite administrative screening and the subsequent provisional designation technique, the process took two years and a half.[8] To have complicated it further by holding hearings on each individual, could well have meant that the whole program would not have progressed beyond the planning stage. (We can only surmise that the suggestion of court hearings with attorneys for prosecution and defense was designed as a delaying tactic.) Again, the additional time, staff, and funds required to effectuate the Japanese proposal could have resulted only in little, if any, substantial changes in the composition of Japan's leadership. This in turn would have had disastrous effects on the over-all objectives of the Occupation.

As is now clear, speed of implementation was of primary consequence to those interested in having the purge be more than a paper reform. In retrospect, it is easy to adopt a posture of indignation concerning

[6] Of considerable interest is the dominant opinion on the part of screening committee members that the designation process should have been completely judicial or at least semijudicial rather than administrative. Tokyo University Social Science Research Institute: *Gyosei Iinkai* (*Administrative Committees*), pp. 145–146. Regrettably, only 32.5 per cent of the prefectural committee members and 42 per cent of the municipal committee members replied to the questionnaires sent out by the study group (*ibid.*, p. 122). Nonetheless, the opinion cited above is believed to be fairly representative, being confirmed by personal conversations.

[7] This decision, on the basis of available records, was never officially or consciously taken. The whole pattern of the purge program, however, indicates that (as far as SCAP personnel were concerned) the criteria were paramount, and that implementation was secondary.

[8] January 4, 1946, to May 10, 1948. This period does not include subsequent additions to the ultranationalist societies category nor the designation of the Communist party leadership.

the removal of individuals from public life purely on the basis of past acts and associations without opportunity for appeal. The enormity of the task must be remembered, however. Under the terms of the initial directive, close to nine thousand holders of, or applicants for, positions in public life were screened.[9] By May, 1948, the careers of well over nine hundred thousand individuals had been checked in order to determine their eligibility.[10] During the entire course of the program, "Questionnaires of over one and a half million persons were examined. Eight hundred and twenty officials, assisted by thousands of assistants, conducted the screening."[11] Furthermore, the extensive (in fact, possibly excessive) study and research which went into the formulation of the purge criteria must be recalled.

Practical problems justified the use of the administrative rather than the judicial process in implementing the purge. Yet the Occupation was also trying to implant concepts of Anglo-Saxon justice and respect for individual liberties.[12] Any occupation would ultimately have to face numerous such paradoxes; this was particularly true in the Occupation of Japan.

No program such as the purge would have been necessary if the dominant members of the various elites which controlled the Japanese government had been angels (to paraphrase Mr. Madison). As it was, the then dominant *Shimpoto* (Progressive party)[13] had asked its members in November, 1945, to search their own souls to determine the extent of their "war guilt."

Designation Procedures

Three separate groups in the Japanese government conducted a review of "public office"[14] holders and applicants during 1946. The first group consisted of the chief of the Cabinet Secretariat and "other offi-

[9] SCAPIN 550, *loc. cit.*, and its implementing Japanese Government Imperial Ordinance No. 109, February 28, 1946. By January 4, 1947, 8,899 persons had been screened. A total of 8,920 individuals were checked for eligibility before beginning the purge's implementation on the basis of the so-called extension ordinances. *PRJ*, Vol. I, p. 29.

[10] 717,415 screened plus 193,180 provisionally designated, making a total of 910,595. *PRJ*, Vol. II, p. 553.

[11] "Control of Anti-Democratic Elements," p. 15.

[12] Cf. "The Judicial and Legal System," *PRJ*, Vol. I, pp. 186–245.

[13] The party was "progressive" in terms of the situation as it existed in the 1880's. After several changes in appellation, its members have ended up in the present Liberal-Democratic party.

[14] Definition of "public office" and its implications on the effectiveness of the purge are discussed below, pp. 62–65.

cials of the Cabinet and of the Home Ministry."[15] The sole task of this group was to examine the qualifications of candidates for the first postwar general election scheduled for April, 1946. Not all applicants who were affected by the purge criteria were designated. Instead, these potential purgees were allowed to withdraw their candidacy voluntarily or were not issued certificates of eligibility.[16] Difficulties developed from this lack of designation because surveillance agencies were unable to restrict the political activities of the potential purgees.

A second committee was established subsequent to the issuance of the imperial ordinance translating the terms of the purge directive (SCAPIN 550) into Japanese law.[17] Again the chief of the Cabinet Secretariat was chairman. Aside from Chairman Narahashi Wataru, the committee members were all career bureaucrats. The members included the director of the Legislative Bureau, deputy chief of the Central Liaison Office (that is, the former foreign ministry), and the vice-ministers of Home Affairs, Justice, Education, and Commerce and Industry.[18] This committee had two crucial tasks. First, it prepared the March 10 and May 16 interpretations of the initial purge directive. These interpretations spelled out into specific categories the broad classification "additional militarists and ultranationalists" (category G of SCAPIN 550) and made minor adjustments in the purge criteria affecting "officers of financial and development organizations involved in Japanese expansion" (category E of SCAPIN 550).[19] In being able to guide the formulation of these interpretations, especially those of category G, this committee was in an excellent position to protect a group in which they had a vested interest, namely, the bureaucracy.

One example illustrates the power at the committee's disposal. A clause of the so-called civil liberties directive, under which all political prisoners had been freed and the Japanese government had been ordered to remove restrictions on political, civil, and religious liberties, had ordered the removal of the entire personnel of the Special Higher Police from "the Ministry of Home Affairs, the Ministry of Justice or any police organ in Japan."[20] These officials, who had come

[15] "The Development of the Affairs concerning the Purge from Public Office" (hereafter "DAPPO"), p. 2. Narahashi Wataru was chief cabinet secretary at that time (spring of 1946). One year later the Central Screening Committee, composed of Premier Yoshida Shigeru appointees, purged Narahashi.

[16] "DAPPO," p. 2.

[17] Imperial Ordinance No. 109, February 28, 1946.

[18] "DAPPO," pp. 2–3.

[19] *PRJ*, Vol. I, pp. 21–23; 27–28.

[20] SCAPIN 93, October 4, 1945, paragraph 1b, "Removal of Restrictions of Political, Civil and Religious Liberties." *PRJ*, Vol. II, p. 464.

closest to being a Japanese equivalent of the Gestapo and who had been charged with protecting the Japanese people from "dangerous thoughts," were not to be reappointed to positions in the Ministries of Home Affairs and Justice. All other positions in the government were open to them under the provisions of the above directive.[21] Their inclusion under the terms of the purge directive, given the broad criterion concerning "any person who has denounced or contributed to the seizure of opponents of the militarist regime,"[22] could be considered a matter of course. The March 10 interpretation of category G, instead of listing as purgeable "the entire personnel," read as follows: "Any person who has a service record of over four years since March, 1941, or over eight years with the Special Higher Police, and who occupied the position of inspector or above during such periods."[23] Two specifications narrowed the possible impact of the criterion. One was the requirement that the official concerned would have served for the entire war period or for a total period of eight years, both of which were highly unlikely qualifications in view of the Japanese bureaucratic practice of shifting personnel from one department to another. The second was that these lengthy periods of service had to be spent in the rank of police inspector. These qualifications so restricted this particular criterion that its impact was negligible.[24]

The second task of this cabinet committee was to screen all high officials in the various ministries. These *Chokunin* rank (i.e., first class) officials had submitted questionnaires to their respective department ministers who had prescreened them. These questionnaires contained the following data: (1) title of position for which person was to be screened; (2) record of employment or military service; (3) membership in organizations, especially in the Imperial Rule societies or ultranationalistic associations; (4) writings and speeches; (5) corporate positions held; (6) and any additional remarks to clarify the entries.[25] The individual was required to sign a statement that all entries were correct and that he understood it to be a criminal offense to omit relevant information or to make false entries. The sanction behind this provision was "penal servitude or imprisonment for less than one year

[21] For example, one special higher police official ended up in the position of liaison official between a prefectural government and a military government team.

[22] SCAPIN 550, Appendix A, category G, paragraph 1. *PRJ*, Vol. I, p. 485.

[23] "March 10th Interpretation of Category G," paragraph 4c, *PRJ*, Vol. I, p. 23.

[24] So negligible, in fact, that the detailed summary of purge statistics does not include them in a separate category. *PRJ*, Vol. II, pp. 554–564.

[25] For the format of a questionnaire, cf. *PRJ*, Vol. II, pp. 486–489.

or a fine of less than 3,000 yen."[26] Complete surveillance by the Occupation was very difficult because of the paucity of information available to SCAP personnel. The cabinet screening committee, with its bureaucratic composition, could not be expected to provide the adequate supervision needed to implement the provision effectively.

The third committee which screened public officials during 1946 came into existence in June.[27] It was chaired by Professor Minobe Tatsukichi who, in spite of his troubles with the military during the 1930's over his "emperor as an organ of state" theory, had become a member of the Privy Council in the postwar period. New blood was also provided by Baba Tsunego, then president of the *Yomiuri Shimbun,* and Irumano Takeo, president of the Teikoku bank (a Mitsui affiliate). Membership on the committee was rounded out by Vice Minister of Foreign Affairs Terasaki Taro, Vice Minister of Home Affairs Iinuma Iisho, and Vice Minister of Justice Tanimura Iichiro. This committee was again heavily weighted in favor of the bureaucracry, with only Baba and Irumano representing other interests.

During 1946, these committees designated 1,067 individuals from a total of 8,920 public office holders screened.[28] This record was attained primarily because of the categorical character of the criteria. If the criteria had been defined only in general terms, two eventualities could have resulted. Either the criteria would have been interpreted out of existence (as in the case of the former officials in the Special Higher Police), or the purgers would have been overly lenient in their application of the criteria to members of the vested interest groups. To have relied on the discretion of these particular groups of purgers would have meant giving up any hope for effective compliance with the purge directive. This also illustrates the inattention to administrative implementation initially displayed by SCAP.

---

[26] Article VIII, Imperial Ordinance No. 109, p. 3. At the time the article was formulated the official exchange rate was fifteen yen to the dollar, so that even if the courts had enforced the penal provision (which they did not do during 1946) the equivalent of $200 would not have been prohibitive. This article was the outcome of SCAPIN 550, paragraph 17. "Willful falsification of or failure to make full and complete disclosures in any Questionnaire, Report or Application provided for in this directive will be punishable by SCAP as a violation of the Surrender Terms. In addition, the Imperial Japanese Government will make any provisions necessary to provide adequate punishment in Japanese courts under Japanese law for such willful falsification or non-disclosure and will undertake such prosecutions as may be required."

[27] Imperial Ordinance No. 346, June 29, 1946.

[28] Summary of 1946 purge statistics. *PRJ,* Vol. I, p. 29.

The 1947–1948 Screening Committees

Many shortcomings of the initial administrative process designed to implement the purge were overcome after the purge criteria were expanded in January, 1947. The previous haphazard approach was formalized to handle the heavier load of screening. Three levels of committees were established. At the apex was the central screening committee (technically entitled the "Central Public Office Qualifications Examination Committee").[29] At the next tier were forty-six prefectural and metropolitan area (*To, Do, Fu,* and *Ken*) committees. In addition, each city (118 in all) with a population of more than 50,000 had its own municipal screening committee. Each committee's jurisdiction was legally established,[30] with detailed points of jurisdiction spelled out in an appendix to the law.[31] Depending on the jurisdictional level, the prime minister or prefectural governor made the official designation and publicized the action taken.[32] The municipal committees reported their recommendations to the prefectural committee; in turn, it reported to the central committee, which could postreview actions taken at the prefectural level.[33] Nine members composed the central committee, and each prefectural and municipal committee had five members. If any committee became overburdened, temporary committee members might be appointed. These members, however, did not have the right to vote.[34] For transacting official business, a quorum of five members for the central committee and three for the lower level committees was established. Decisions were made on the basis of majority vote; in case of a tie the chairman was allowed to vote twice.[35] Each committee was also provided with a secretariat to assist members in doing research and taking care of administrative matters.[36]

This elaborate administrative machinery accomplished two tasks. First, all holders of public office and persons applying for positions in public life (e.g., candidates for various elections), were screened. Any

[29] Imperial Ordinance No. 2, January 4, 1947, Article I, *PRJ,* Vol. II, p. 505.
[30] Imperial Ordinance No. 2, January 4, 1947, Article II, *PRJ,* Vol. II, p. 505.
[31] Cabinet and Home Ministry Ordinance No. 1, January 4, 1947, Appendix III. *PRJ,* Vol. II, pp. 543–544.
[32] Imperial Ordinance No. 2, January 4, 1947, Articles VI and VII. *PRJ,* Vol. II, pp. 505–506.
[33] Imperial Ordinance No. 2, January 4, 1947, Articles III, IV, and V. *PRJ,* Vol. II, p. 505.
[34] Imperial Ordinance No. 2, January 4, 1947, Article VIII. *PRJ,* Vol. II, p. 506.
[35] Imperial Ordinance No. 2, January 4, 1947, Article X. *PRJ,* Vol. II, p. 506.
[36] Imperial Ordinance No. 2, January 4, 1947, Articles XII and XIII. *PRJ,* Vol. II, p. 506. These articles were added to Imperial Ordinance No. 2, by Imperial Ordinance No. 64 of March 3, 1947. *PRJ,* Vol. II, p. 546. Initially, little thought had apparently been given to the clerical help each committee would need.

individual who fitted into either of these groups submitted a questionnaire to the appropriate screening committee. Based on a review of his career, he received either a certificate of eligibility or notification that he had been designated a purgee. Second, the screening committee undertook the process of provisionally designating all purgees. In effect, this procedure reversed the screening process. Initially, only the careers of persons in (or aspiring to positions in) public life were reviewed by the screening committees. Under the provisional designation program, however, any individual could be provisionally designated, providing that either the prime minister or prefectural governor had "reasonable evidence" that he had held a position or engaged in activities proscribed by the purge criteria.[37] This provisional designation program was at first effectuated by means of the prime minister or prefectural governor's asking the individual to submit a questionnaire to the appropriate screening committee.[38]

As the provisional designation program began to get under way, procedures were further simplified in a cabinet order amending the basic ordinance.[39] It established the following procedures: (1) if sufficient evidence existed as a matter of public record, the prime minister or prefectural governors could designate an individual as a purgee even without a questionnaire; (2) a person so designated had the opportunity to file with the appropriate screening committee any material which he believed would serve as counterevidence; (3) this counterevidence had to be submitted within a period of thirty days from the date of his designation. At first a formal letter or telegram informed each individual of his designation. In the end, designation was made by the publication of lists in the *Official Gazette*.[40] The difference in

[37] Imperial Ordinance No. 77, March 12, 1947, which amended Article IV of Imperial Ordinance No. 1 of January 4, 1947. *PRJ*, Vol. II, p. 501. Originally, Article IV had read, "The designation of a person who holds or is a candidate applicant for public office as a person who falls under the Memorandum shall be effected . . . in accordance with the result of examination by the Public Office Examination Committee." Imperial Ordinance No. 77 expanded this article to include the following provision, "Besides persons mentioned above, the Prime Minister or the Prefectural Governor, based upon reasonable evidence that a person is subject to the provisions of the Memorandum, may, on the basis of the findings of the Public Office Qualifications Committee, designate him as falling under the Memorandum in accordance with a rule laid down by the Prime Minister."

[38] "In connection with designation provided in Article IV [quoted in footnote 37], the Prime Minister or the prefectural governor shall collect the questionnaire. . . ." Imperial Ordinance No. 1, January 4, 1947, Article VII. *PRJ*, Vol. II, p. 501.

[39] Cabinet Order No. 119, July 2, 1947. Its provisions are contained in Articles VII–II and VII–III of Imperial Ordinance No. 2, January 4, 1947. *PRJ*, Vol. II, pp. 501–502.

[40] *PRJ*, Vol. I, pp. 43–44. Cabinet Order No. 237, November 7, 1947, provided that the governors were responsible for designating local officials of the Imperial Rule Societies and the Imperial Ex-Servicemen's Association (*Zaigo Gunjin Kai*).

impact between the screening and provisional designation processes in determining who was a purgee can be noted in the following statistics. Of the 201,815 purgees, 8,635 were determined by the screening process (hence, were holders of, or applicants for, public office at the time), whereas 193,180 were included by the provisional designation process.

Summary of Designation Procedures

A basic shift in the administration of the purge took place with the utilization of the provisional designation program. This program began by screening individuals who were in or were aspiring to positions of authority in public life. As a result, many potential purgees either withdrew from official positions, accepted positions in which they were not screenable, or stayed in the background completely. The program ended by taking the criteria as points of departure and designating all individuals who were affected by them. The screening process used the purge criteria as guidelines within which some leeway of interpretation could be granted, but the provisional designation process froze the criteria and made automatic the purge designation of anyone who fell within their scope. Thus the provisional designation process was considerably quicker and more efficient. Had it been used from the inception of the administrative implementation, there would not have been the confusion of who really was or was not a purgee. The whole burden of this determination was placed on the purge criteria instead of on the shoulders of the screening committee members. The elaborate structure of screening committees was superfluous for the designation of more than 95 per cent of the total number of purgees. Whatever administrative efficiency was gained by use of the provisional designation process, it compromised any attempts to add flexibility to the administration of the purge. It was the administrative technique most suited to the purge criteria as finally formulated. To the extent that the purge criteria became ever more specific, to that extent an elaborate administrative mechanism to implement them became unnecessary. Yet the role the screening committees played was significant. Only by looking at their membership and the work they accomplished can insight be gained into their usefulness in implementing a program like the purge.

Political Influences on the Screening Committees

The preponderance of bureaucrats on the cabinet committees which supervised the administration of the purge during 1946 has been noted.[41] Since the primary emphasis in implementing the purge during that

[41] *Supra*, pp. 45–48.

year was on the bureaucracy, the Japanese government, by appointments to these committees, insured that this group was adequately protected. To be sure, whatever protection the committee members could provide was limited by the categorical character of the purge criteria.

If protecting certain groups was a motivating factor in the minds of those who made the appointments, what interest groups were represented on the 1947–1948 central screening committee? Matsushima Shikao, a former career diplomat (i.e., foreign office bureaucrat) who had close family ties with the zaibatsu, was the first chairman of the central screening committee. In his diplomatic capacity, he had served during World War II as a member of the German-Japanese-Italian Mixed Technical Committee. His close ties to the dominant Liberal party (Yoshida was premier at the time of his appointment), is evidenced by his presidency of the *Naigai Shimbun,* which became the semiofficial organ of that party.[42] During Matsushima's chairmanship, the Democratic party, which had been organized out of the remnants of the Progressive party and whose organizers intended to challenge Liberal party dominance in the conservative camp, lost four of its executive committee members via the purge. First to be designated was Narahashi Wataru.[43] He was quickly followed by Inukai Ken, Ishiguro Takeshige, and Chizaki Usaburo. Understandably, the Democrats proclaimed that the screening committee was politically motivated. In answer, the official purge history somewhat piously notes that Matsuoka Matsuhei, a member of the Liberal party, was designated at the same time.[44] Matsushima remained as chairman until June, when the Socialists and Democrats, who had formed a coalition cabinet subsequent to the general election held in April, had their way by insisting that an individual with less partisan political ties should serve as chairman.

Makino Eiichi was appointed June 30 as the new chairman. He had been professor of law at Tokyo (Imperial) University and also had been a government official, first as a public procurator and later as a judge of the Tokyo District Court and counselor of the Cabinet Legislative Bureau. Makino's career indicates that his ties with the bureaucracy were reasonably close.[45]

[42] Information is based on data in Matsushima's questionnaire.

[43] *Supra,* p. 46. Narashashi was among the first to have his purge designation canceled by the appeals board in May, 1948. *PRJ*, Vol. I, p. 40, note **. Interestingly enough, Ashida Hitoshi, a Democrat, was prime minister at that time.

[44] *PRJ*, Vol. I, p. 40.

[45] Makino Eiichi, questionnaire on file in Cabinet Secretariat.

Of the other eight committee members, two were established journalists, Kato Masuo and Iwabuchi Tatsuo. Kato, a graduate of the University of Chicago, had been a foreign correspondent whose prewar career was climaxed by his four-year service as head of the Domei News Agency's Washington bureau. Since the war, he has been one of the managing editors of the Kyodo News Service and has achieved international renown for his book on wartime Japan, *The Lost War.*[46] Iwabuchi, one of the foremost political critics of Japan (comparable in stature to Walter Lippmann in the United States), had been twice arrested during the 1930's for criticizing the army. Interestingly enough, he was politically close to Hatoyama Ichiro as well as to General Masaki, one of the leaders of the "Kodoha." He is also reputed to have been a member of Prince Konoye's "brain trust."[47] Kimura Kozaemon, a member of the Liberal Party, represented the Diet of which he was vice-speaker at the time.[48] He resigned concurrently with Matsushima's departure from the chairmanship. Shirogane Tomonori, a lifelong bureaucrat, was his replacement. Labor was represented by Miki Jiro, who at the time was president of the Steel Cable and Line-Workers Union. Subsequent to his election to the House of Representatives in April, 1947, his place on the committee was taken by Kumamoto Torazo, long-time Socialist and at the time member of the Social Democratic party's central executive committee. Hara Yasusaburo represented industry during the entire existence of the committee. He had been a successful executive in various enterprises which included the manufacture of gunpowder. A dynamic man, he acquired the reputation of being among the fair-minded committee members, impervious to political pressure. The academic world had Okouchi Kazuo as its spokesman. A professor of economics at Tokyo (Imperial) University, his wide range of talents had also been enlisted by the ministers of finance, education, and welfare in the solution of social problems. The committee was rounded out by two lawyers, Shono Riichi and Unno Shinkichi. Shono was subsequently appointed to the first Supreme Court in which position he achieved some notoriety by accusing Chairman Makino of activities prejudicial to the committee's reputation.[49]

[46] A highly personal account of the era between Japan's last diplomatic peace efforts before Pearl Harbor and her ultimate defeat.

[47] Iwabuchi Tatsuo, questionnaire on file in Cabinet Secretariat.

[48] The data for this section are drawn from the questionnaires of the individuals concerned, *PRJ*, Vol. I, p. 36, and personal knowledge.

[49] Shono accused Makino of having received a bribe (from unnamed sources, but implying from SCAP) for reversing the screening committee's decision in the case of Hirano Rikizo, Minister of Agriculture and Forestry in the Katayama cabinet. For other aspects of the Hirano case, cf. *infra,* pp. 54–57.

Unno, during World War II, had had the courage to act as defense counsel for persons accused of thought-control violations. Subsequent to his service on the screening committee, of which he was considered the most conscientious member by its secretariat, he became president of the Japan Civil Liberties Union.

In assessing the character of the committee, two factors need to be kept in mind. The prime minister, who was the appointing authority in the Japanese government,[50] would have been negligent in his duty were he not to try to protect groups upon which he was politically dependent. Premier Yoshida could count on Matsushima, Iwabuchi, and Kimura to provide a hard core of support necessitating that only two of the other six members vote in line to provide the necessary majority. By the same token, the Socialist-Democratic coalition cabinet under the leadership of Katayama Tetsu changed the complexion of the committee to bring its membership into closer conformity with the cabinet's political interests. A second factor influencing the composition of the committee was that the purge became the object of countless attacks on the score that it was the tool of "leftists" in general and Communists in particular.[51] Given these considerations, it is perhaps easier to understand the complexion of the committee. Even more remarkable is the relative degree to which a reasonable balance of forces representing Japanese society was attained.

To be sure, the Japanese screening committee worked within the context of two severe limitations on its power. The first of these was the detailed nature of the criteria. The supervision exercised by SCAP served as the second limiting factor, for despite the small number (112, of which 39 were subsequently revoked)[52] of cases which were officially overruled by SCAP, a necessarily close coördination was maintained between the central screening committee and Government Section. The administrative problems encountered can best be examined by reviewing a particular case.

The Hirano Case

Hirano Rikizo served as Minister of Agriculture and Forestry in the Katayama Tetsu (Socialist-Democratic coalition) cabinet from May,

---

[50] Imperial Ordinance No. 2, January 4, 1947, Article IX. *PRJ*, Vol. II, p. 506.

[51] The official history of the purge explains the committee membership as follows: "An effort was made by the appointing authorities to enlist the services of individuals who had achieved prominence in their chosen professions and who would bring to the committee a broad knowledge of various fields of activity. . . . Similarly on the prefectural level the governors sought to select prominent persons whose integrity could not be questioned. . . ." *PRJ*, Vol. I, p. 36.

[52] "Control of Anti-Democratic Elements," *op. cit.*, p. 10.

1947, until January, 1948. Shortly after his graduation from Waseda University in 1922, he had started on his lifelong career as a leader in agrarian reform movements. His first official position was as a member of the Propaganda Section and subsequently a prefectural director of the Japan Farmers' Union. His differences with the main trend of this organization (which he believed to be leftist) began as early as 1926 and ended in 1930 with his helping to organize the rival All Japan Farmers' Union, of which he became president two years later—a position he held until 1939. Politically, he had participated in founding the Japan Farmers' party (*Nippon Nomin To*) in 1926, the next year joining forces with the Japan Masses party (*Nippon Taishu To*). Five years later, he joined the Japan National Socialist party (*Nippon Kokka Shakai To*) but left to establish the Imperial Way Society (*Kodo Kai*) in 1933. He was elected to the House of Representatives in the 1937 general election as a candidate of the Imperial Way Society and was reëlected in the 1942 wartime election without the recommendation of the Tojo cabinet. He helped to organize the Socialist party in the fall of 1945 and did yeoman service for it in agricultural communities. During the culmination of his political career, after having served as agriculture and forestry minister for eight months, he was designated as a purgee by the central screening committee on January 13, 1948.[53]

What were the official reasons for his designation? First, Hirano, in helping to establish the Japan National Socialist party, "bears out that both in action and ideology he injected fascistic thoughts into the agrarian movement."[54] Also, his appointment as standing director and central committee member of the Japan National Socialism Study League in which Okawa Shumei (an ideologue of Japanese nationalism who gained international renown by tapping Tojo on the head in the war crimes trials) was a leading member and which maintained close contact with the Great Japan Production party (*Dai Nippon Seisan To*), indicated "the ideological tendency of Hirano."[55] Most significant for the committee, however, was Hirano's association with the Imperial Way Society (*Kodo Kai*). This organization "aimed at the farm mili-

[53] Biographical data is from Hirano Rikizo's questionnaire, on file in the Cabinet Secretariat.

[54] A Japanese press release noted, "Based on the examination report by the Central Public Office Qualification Examination Committee on 13 January, 1948, the Prime Minister has made decision [*sic*] that Rikizo Hirano falls under Category G of the purge ordinance." [Japanese] *Government Announcement*, January 13, 1948. Separate copy, mimeo., p. 1.

[55] *Ibid.*, p. 2.

tary solidarity and the establishment of the Imperial Way Government (*Kodo Seiji*). . . . He was one of the influential founders of the *Kodo Kai*. . . . He was at once the editor and publisher of the magazine *Kodo,* official organ of the society over the period ranging from 7 July, 1937, to 7 December, 1941."[56]

That this case against Hirano was not all it might have been from the viewpoint of the purge criteria is indicated by the committee vote. At its meeting of December 26, 1947, the committee voted five to four to clear Hirano. Two weeks later, again by five to four vote, this previous "temporary decision"[57] was reversed. The committee vote, presumably secret, had been leaked to the press.[58] One of the sources for this leak was Hirano himself, who saw to it that a letter, addressed to him by committee member Okouchi and written at the request of Mrs. Hirano, received wide publicity. Professor Okouchi, in this letter, had stated that he had reversed his previous vote clearing Hirano only after receiving assurance from Chairman Makino that unanimity prevailed among the other committee members (with the exception of Iwabuchi Tatsuo) favoring Hirano's designation as a purgee. On the basis of this understanding, Okouchi changed his vote, thereby bringing about Hirano's removal from politics. The committee's behavior does not make sense unless we take into account the fact that dating back to May, 1947, Government Section had been pressing the screening committee to purge Hirano. A letter directive ordering his removal from public office was prepared but never sent.[59]

Whatever the merits of Hirano's designation as a purgee—and on this, legitimate differences of opinion exist—the administrative procedure was confusing. The Japanese government was forced to take responsibility for an action it did not wish to take. Political repercussions shook public confidence in the purge and added fuel to the charges that it was a tool for those Japanese in control of its administration to rid themselves of political rivals; in reality it was SCAP that was doing the manipulating. Had it not been for the policy to make the Japanese government seem solely responsible for the administration of the purge, and had SCAP simply issued a directive, much of the

[56] *Ibid.*, pp. 2–4.

[57] Makino Eiichi, "Announcement," January 13, 1948, separate copy, mimeo.

[58] *Mainichi Shimbun,* January 20, 1948. The secrecy provision of the purge ordinance read as follows: "The Chairman, Commissioners and Temporary Commissioners shall neither publish nor disclose any information concerning matters connected with the official duties of the Committee. . . ." Imperial Ordinance No. 2, January 4, 1947, Article XI. *PRJ,* Vol. II, p. 506.

[59] Personal knowledge.

harm that this case did to the purge could have been avoided. Arguments about the merits of Hirano's purge would no doubt have continued. However, at least responsibility for the decision would have been clear, and the work of the screening committee would not have been compromised. In the final analysis, the committee did accomplish the major share of its work independently, with SCAP personnel entering the administrative process only on certain occasions. One was the Hatoyama case. Had the Hirano case been handled in like fashion, much pain and anguish could have been spared certain members of the screening committee.[60]

From a general point of view, this case illustrates the difficulties that can be expected in forcing a government, under the control of a foreign occupation, to undertake the removal of individuals with whom the administrators themselves have close political or personal ties and concurrently to make it seem as if all that was accomplished was done without reference to the wishes of alien forces. This approach might be feasible under the cloak of absolute secrecy. For as complex and far-flung an administrative structure as that which controlled the purge, such an attempt could only lead to public confusion and disaffection.[61]

Appeals

Except for the brief notation that a provisional designee could file counterevidence with the appropriate screening committee, no reference has been made to any procedures whereby a purgee could appeal his designation. Shortly after issuance of SCAPIN 550, General Whitney clarified Occupation policy on the subject of appeals.

> If compliance with the directive results in inequitable treatment of a few individuals, this can be remedied after compliance is completed. There is no objection to the establishment of a Commission of Inquiry . . . for the purpose of holding hear-

[60] Sone Eki, one of the officials most intimately concerned with the purge and at present a Social Democratic member of the House of Councilors, made the following points to me in an interview: Initially SCAP accepted responsibility in issuing the basic purge directive and in issuing specific memoranda directing the purge of specific individuals. As the program progressed, however, SCAP (specifically Government Section) evaded this "responsibility" by utilizing only indirect pressure. As a result (and he uses the Hirano case as the most important example), the "justice" of the purge was questioned by the people. He asserts that the oral order directing Hirano's removal had as its alternative the order directing the downfall of the cabinet. Cf. also his statement in Sumimoto Toshio, *Senryo Hiroku*, pp. 112–113.

[61] Hirano's designation as a purgee by the Central Screening Committee in January, 1948, did not signal the end of complications. He was subsequently involved in two court cases which were both concerned with his purge status.

ings and making recommendations to the Japanese Government for exemption of certain individuals coming under the directive providing that the individual is first removed from public office in accordance with the directive and providing the action taken by the commission is submitted to SCAP for review prior to reinstatement in public office of any individual removed therefrom.[62]

In spite of the generally haphazard administration, certain individual cases received very careful review. Because of this care and the relatively small number of persons (1,067)[63] purged during 1946, no specific procedures were established for handling appeals. "The few [appeals] that did arise were given individual consideration by the Cabinet and in some cases recommendations for reinstatement were made to SCAP."[64] However, in no case was the purge ruling reversed.

Concomitant with the extension of the purge in January, 1947, a real need arose for the review of individual cases in view of the broader categories and hence wider application of the purge. In answer to this need, a formal appeals procedure was legalized, and an appeals board was established.[65] Guiding the actions of this Appeals Board was the criterion of whether or not an error had been made in the purge designation by the screening committee.[66] The actions of the second appeals board (the first had been abolished May 10, 1948)[67] were governed by the provision that purgees could appeal their designation "if they deem such designation involves gross injustice."[68] Subsequent to its abolition,[69] a third round of appeals was permitted. It was governed by the following provision, "The Prime Minister may, when he finds that the designation as the person who falls under the Memorandum . . . *has come to lack equity* cancel the designation. . . ."[70]

Criteria providing for a gradually increasing scope of discretion guided the consideration of successive appeals. Initially, errors in

[62] Interview with Shidehara: "Memorandum from Chief, Government Section to SCAP," January 25, 1946, as quoted in *PRJ*, Vol. I, p. 18.

[63] *PRJ*, Vol. I, p. 29.

[64] *PRJ*, Vol. I, pp. 41–42.

[65] Imperial Ordinance No. 65, "Appeals Procedure"; and Imperial Ordinance No. 66, "Regulation on Organization of Public Office Qualifications Appeal Board." Both promulgated on March 1, 1947. For texts, cf. *PRJ*, Vol. II, pp. 550–551.

[66] Imperial Ordinance No. 65, March 1, 1947, Article II, *loc. cit.* "Any person who has been designated as falling under the Memorandum . . . may in the event he feels an error has been made in his case and that he can submit proof thereof, file an appeal for a rescission of designation to the Prime Minister."

[67] *PRJ*, Vol. I, p. 42.

[68] Cabinet Order No. 39, February 8, 1949, Article I. *Official Gazette*, Extra No. 14 (Eng. ed.), February 8, 1949, p. 1.

[69] Cabinet Order No. 51, March 28, 1951. *Official Gazette*, No. 1499 (Eng. ed.), March 28, 1951, p. 9.

[70] Cabinet Order No. 220, June 18, 1951. *Official Gazette*, No. 1567 (Eng. ed.), June 18, 1951, p. 4. (Italics mine.)

designation were to be considered. The question of whether or not the criteria actually applied to the person designated was to be the sole consideration, for example, if a person listed as an officer of a proscribed organization had actually held that position. Subsequently, consideration was to be given to cases involving gross injustice. No definition of this term was provided, but by implication a considerably larger group of purgees would be led to file an appeal and to expect favorable consideration. In both instances, however, the burden of proving the impropriety of the purge designation fell upon the appellant.[71] Under the relevant legal provision guiding the last round of appeals, the reverse approach was employed. The prime minister, guided by principles of his own making (he was not legally bound by any specific criteria), could rescind a purge designation if it had "come to lack equity."[72] With this provision, the cycle of the purge was completed, and its complete rescission, under law, became possible

The successive waves of appeals which were approved made even more manifest the pattern that emerges from the ordinances guiding them. The first appeals board, which lasted from the spring of 1947 to the spring of 1948, considered 1,471 appeals. Of these, 150 were recommended by the appeals board for release from the purge, of which number all but 7 were accepted by SCAP.[73] The second appeals board (February, 1949, to March, 1951) considered 32,089 appeals, of which 10,090 were approved for release from designation. Within one month after the establishment of the third appeals board in June, 1951, 66,025 purgees designated by prefectural and municipal screening committees and 2,958 designated by the central screening committee were released.[74]

Toward the end, the Japanese government could not keep up with SCAP demands to hurry the de-purge process.[75] Partial reason for this was that credit for these acts of magnanimity was at stake. A wide gulf separates these last acts of the Occupation (the Peace Treaty Confer-

[71] Footnote 66, *supra.*

[72] *Supra,* p. 58. Cabinet Order No. 220 of 1951 was one of the products of General Ridgway's May Day (1951) statement authorizing the Japanese government to review existing Japanese laws which had been promulgated as implementations of SCAP directives. Japanese Ministry of Foreign Affairs, *Present Conditions of Japan,* p. 22. (Hereafter PCJ.)

[73] *PRJ,* Vol. I, p. 42.

[74] *PCJ, op. cit.,* p. 22. In addition, 1,522 purgees had been administratively reinstated by the prime minister in the interim period between the first and second Appeals Boards and 3,250 "young ex-officers of the army and navy, none of whom had had any connection with the military service prior to December 8, 1941, and none of whom could be held responsible for leading the Japanese people into World War II" were reinstated in October, 1950. "Control of Anti-Democratic Elements," p. 16.

[75] Private talks with SCAP and Japanese government officials concerned.

ence in San Francisco was held in August and September, 1951) and the supervision exercised by Government Section over the appeals machinery in April, 1947. At the earlier date, when the Japanese government announced the first release of an appellant's designation before SCAP review, General Whitney wrote a stinging letter to Premier Yoshida Shigeru.

> *a.* The Supreme Commander has consistently recognized the propriety of appellate machinery within the Japanese Government to investigate and bring to light any injustice in the application of the Memorandum (SCAPIN 550). Accordingly, *there is no fundamental objection* to the continued existence of the Appeals Board *in a purely advisory capacity.*
>
> *b.* It is desired, however, that no person who has been designated as falling under the Memorandum and thereby removed or barred from the public service be reinstated until his case, with a report of the appellate proceedings, has been submitted to this headquarters for review and prior approval.[76]

Summary

Officially, the appellate machinery had as its objective the "alleviation of inequalities in administration,"[77] certainly a laudable concept to anyone interested in Anglo-Saxon ideas of due process. However, the pattern that emerges from a consideration of the legal principles which guided the successive appeals boards, the actions they took, and the change in supervision exercised by SCAP belies this stated purpose. The appellate machinery, instead of considering errors in designation or cases of gross injustice, became the vehicle for bringing purgees back into public life. In comparison to the elaborateness of the purge criteria which guided the work of the screening committees, the appeals boards operated almost without guidelines. This, in turn, raises a fundamental problem. An example of the diffusion of responsibility, discussed earlier, was the administrative bifurcation between the screening committees and the appeals boards. Without criteria to guide the latter, it is clear that both agencies were essentially operating solely on the basis of the purge criteria. On what basis, therefore, could the two agencies arrive at differing conclusions if the basic facts of an individual case remained the same? The area of discretion available to both commissions was severely limited in any case by the nature of the criteria on the one hand and the supervisory powers of SCAP on the other. In these limiting factors lies the real explanation for the actions taken by the Japanese agencies concerned.

---

[76] *PRJ*, Vol. I, p. 42.

[77] "Control of Anti-Democratic Elements," p. 16.

The administrative structure which implemented the designation and appellate processes of the purge would seem to be out of Gilbert and Sullivan's *The Mikado.* During 1946, extreme attention to detail and careful review of individual cases were expected from committees which were haphazardly constituted and which had comparatively vague and general criteria with which to work. An elaborate screening committee system was in existence in the January, 1947, to May, 1948, period. This far-flung mechanism, manned by a carefully selected committee membership which worked with well-defined criteria, became in the end an automaton provisionally designating anyone who fell under the criteria to the tune of "I've Got a Little List." An initially nonexistent (though promised) appellate machinery, once it was established, was first tied into knots of inactivity, only a little later to become not a commission for the handling of appeals but rather the agency for dismantling the purge. On top of it all, like a brooding omnipresence (though not as dispassionate as that of Justice Holmes), sat the Occupation, its basic policy orientation reversed in midstream.

CHAPTER VI

LIMITATIONS OF THE PURGE

REMOVAL OF A PURGEE'S influence and authority would not be accomplished merely by designating him a purgee. Yet the Potsdam Declaration had directed the elimination of purgees' authority and influence. Determining who the individuals or groups were, by defining the criteria and by designating the individuals, were important steps in the process, but only that. Elimination of their authority and influence was dependent on other factors. The first factor was that the positions from which the purgees were eliminated actually were important posts in public life. This depended on the legal definitions given to the terms "public office" and "government service." Another factor was that once designated, purgees would not be able to continue to exercise their power by means of being "temporarily retained," essentially because of their irreplaceability. Again, limitations on their engaging in activities, defined as influential, would exist in law, and adequate surveillance facilities were available to control their engaging in proscribed activities, thereby enforcing these prohibitions.

PUBLIC OFFICE AND GOVERNMENT SERVICE

So long as the purge criteria were applied only to individuals actually holding positions in public life, designation of purgees could be limited. SCAPIN 550 ordered the removal from public office and the exclusion from government service of all persons affected by the purge criteria.[1] The impact the purge criteria could have was dependent on the definitions of these two terms. During 1946, public office was defined as including all positions filled by those with the rank of *Chokunin* or above, and the principal offices in government corporations.[2] Government service, on the other hand, included all positions in central and local government and other organizations controlled by the government.[3] An indi-

[1] SCAPIN 550, paragraph 2, *PRJ*, Vol. II, p. 482.

[2] SCAPIN 550, paragraph 3, *PRJ*, Vol. II, p. 482. "The term 'public office' as used in this directive shall mean and include: a. Any position in the government service which is customarily filled by one with the civil service rank of *Chokunin* or above . . . ; or b. Any other position in the government service not customarily filled by a member of the civil service which is equivalent or superior to the civil service rank of *Chokunin* (in the case of government corporations the term will include at least: Chairman of the Board of Directors, President, Vice-President, Director, Advisor, Auditor").

[3] SCAPIN 550, paragraph 4, *PRJ*, Vol. II, p. 482. "The term 'government service' as used in this directive shall mean and include all positions in the central Japanese and Prefectural Governments and all of their agencies and local branches, bureaus . . . and offices and all positions in corporations, associations, and other organizations in which said governments or any of their agencies have a financial interest representing actual or working control."

vidual designated as a purgee was to be removed from his position if it were commensurate with the *Chokunin* civil service rank. Once designated as purgees, however, they could not hold any positions in the whole of the Japanese governmental framework.

The reader will have noted that public office was defined as including only civil servants of *Chokunin* rank. Originally, however, a draft of SCAPIN 550 had specified that public office should include *Sonin* rank bureaucrats. At issue were two problems: whether the *Sonin* rank officials should be considered as having had policy-making responsibility, and whether, by including *Sonin* rank officials for possible removal, Japan's administrative machinery would be denuded of an excessively large group of expert personnel. On the first point the initial choice of the *Sonin* rank was explained as follows:

> The *Sonin* rank . . .was selected, as that rank in the lowest of the three top grades of civil service in Japan. All officials of these grades would have policy-making responsibility in any position to which they might be appointed. The two highest ranks (*Chokunin* and *Shinnin*) are appointed by the Emperor and persons of these ranks may hold positions of Minister, of Privy Counsellor, Judge, etc. The *Sonin* rank usually fills such posts as secretary of a bureau or chief of a section. The appointment is subject to Imperial approval. The effect of the order therefore will be to remove only the highest group of responsible officials in any branch of government service who fall within the disqualifying categories.[4]

The decision not to include *Sonin* rank officials in the definition of public office provides evidence of the caution which guided the SCAP formulators of the purge program, even in its initial stages. Only a part of the "highest group of responsible officials"[5] in the government were affected by the initial criteria.

The effect of this change in the definition of what constituted public office is not difficult to establish. So long as the process of determining who was a purgee depended on screening, all *Sonin* rank officials who were potential purgees could remain in office. This limitation was carried over into the ordinances which expanded the purge program by defining public office into "principal" and "ordinary" categories. "Any person who falls under the provisions of Appendix A to the Memorandum [i.e., the purge criteria], in case he holds any principal public office, *shall* and, in case he holds any *ordinary* public office, *may* be removed therefrom."[6] Only government officials "holding the civil

---

[4] "Memorandum" from Government Section to the Office of the Chief of Staff, Dec. 5, 1945, as quoted in *PRJ*, Vol. I, p. 12.

[5] *Ibid.*

[6] Imperial Ordinance No. 1, January 4, 1947, Article III. *PRJ*, Vol. II, p. 501 (italics mine).

service rank of First Grade or above and those commensurate with the above rank" were included in the principal public office category.[7] Hence, a bureaucrat, even though designated as a purgee, could remain in his position so long as his rank was classified under the ordinary public office category.

This same distinction was made for all other positions classified as public office. For example, in economic organizations, "principal public office" included the chairman or president through standing auditor, whereas "ordinary public office" included auditors, advisors, councilors, and other "highest ranking persons."[8] In newspaper companies, principal public office included also such positions as editor in chief, chief of editorial staff, and news editor in addition to the normal business offices, whereas correspondents, reporters, and others were relegated to holding only ordinary public office.[9]

One interesting category of public office includes officials in the political parties. Diet members (and therefore candidates for Diet membership) were listed as principal public office holders.[10] Initially, however, Japanese political party leaders had contended that purgees should be allowed to retain their party positions. An "opinion" issued by the cabinet brought holders of party offices within the definition of public office.[11] Such positions as advisor, councilor, and auditor remained as ordinary public office in the new ordinance.[12] Furthermore, only political parties which had representation in the Diet were listed.[13] To be sure, in all instances, purgees could remain in their ordinary public office positions only if they held them at the time of screening. No purgees could be appointed to a position listed as public office, regardless of whether it was of the principal or ordinary variety.[14]

The categories defining the scope of what constituted positions of authority and influence were the source of constant difficulties. As has been indicated, the Japanese were at first not ready to include political

[7] Cabinet and Home Ministry Ordinance No. 1, January 4, 1947, Appendix II, paragraph 1. *PRJ*, Vol. II, p. 528. (Under Civil Service Reforms, the old *Shinnin* and *Chokunin* ranks were combined into the "First Grade" rank. Cf. "Civil Service," *PRJ*, Vol. I, pp. 246–259.)

[8] Cabinet and Home Ministry Ordinance No. 1, January 4, 1947, Appendix II, paragraphs 6, 7, 8, 11 and 12. *PRJ*, Vol. II, pp. 529–530; 538–542.

[9] *Ibid.*, paragraph 9, *PRJ*, Vol. II, pp. 531–532.

[10] *Ibid.*, paragraph 2, *PRJ*, Vol. II, p. 528.

[11] *PRJ*, Vol. I, p. 25.

[12] Cabinet and Home Ministry Ordinance No. 1, January 4, 1947, Appendix II, paragraph 10. *PRJ*, Vol. II, p. 537.

[13] *Ibid.*

[14] Imperial Ordinance No. 1, January 4, 1947, Article III, paragraph 3, "Any person who falls under the Memorandum shall be excluded thereafter from any position in the public service." *PRJ*, Vol. II, p. 502.

party offices under its terms. Purgees who had been removed from the Diet could thereby continue to dictate party policies and strategy. To be fully effective, the definition of what constituted public office would have had to be continuously under study and revision. Otherwise, as new agencies, commissions, corporations, and parties became established, purgees could readily return to positions of influence which, however, were not specifically listed as public office. Furthermore, Japanese government compliance was not always forthcoming. Examples are legion, but two will suffice. In the spring of 1946, thirty new appointees filled vacancies in the House of Peers. None was screened until a memorandum directing the Japanese government to do so had been dispatched by SCAP.[15] As late as the spring of 1950, a substantial group of officials in the Ministry of International Trade and Industry was found not to have been screened. They were all, according to the government, "day laborers" who had been appointed "without regard to the provisions of the Law for the Fixed Number of Personnel in Administrative Organs."[16] Investigations revealed that 623,296 such day laborers were to be found in the government, of whom 7,000 were employed more than nine out of ten working days a year. Among them, 139 purgees were found.[17]

Temporary Retentions

One clause of SCAPIN 550 envisaged one group of purgees legally continuing to exercise their influence. "Removals may be postponed in the case of individuals who are absolutely required to insure demobilization of the Japanese armed forces. . . ."[18] Career military and naval officers administered almost the entire demobilization program. These military service personnel were, of course, all purgees. Their services, however, were not limited to aiding the process of demobilization. General Willoughby, the assistant chief of staff for intelligence, employed some of them to help in the preparation of a military history concerning major campaigns of World War II.[19] This special staff of the defunct Imperial Japanese Army general and field grade officers and their naval counterparts received special dispensation in the form of Occupation transportation, food allotments, and the like;

[15] *PRJ*, Vol. I, pp. 24–25.

[16] "Control of Anti-Democratic Elements," p. 5.

[17] *Ibid.*

[18] SCAPIN 550, paragraph 8. *PRJ*, Vol. II, p. 482.

[19] Details concerning this "history" are still fragmentary. Cf. Harry Emerson Wildes, *Typhoon in Tokyo*, pp. 307–309.

this was not well received by those Japanese people who knew about it.[20] Retention of these purgees, both within the framework of the Japanese government and within one of the general staff sections of SCAP, also illustrates problems of control resulting from one of the divisions of responsibility within the Occupation, which hampered the implementation of the purge.[21]

Japanese ordinances implementing SCAPIN 550 expanded upon the directive's permission to grant temporary retentions to personnel other than those needed to aid in demobilization. "When it is impossible to obtain a suitable replacement, [a purgee] . . . may . . . be temporarily retained or reinstated in the principal or ordinary office in accordance with the rule laid down by the Prime Minister. . . . [Any such person] shall be defined, for the term of his approved retention or reinstatement . . . *not* to be a person who falls under the Memorandum."[22] Under the terms of this article, temporary retentions were granted not only to ex-career military officers, but also to politicians, bureaucrats, and industrialists who were the indispensable men in their respective organizations. For these men, removals were deferred only for a specified period of time, which was not the case for demobilization personnel. Four of the ministers in the Shidehara cabinet who were designated as purgees in February, 1946, for example, retained their portfolios until after the first postwar general election (April, 1946).[23] A blanket temporary retention order made it possible for all purgees who were to be designated under the expansion of the purge criteria formulated in the fall of 1946, to remain in office until after the second general election (April, 1947). Furthermore, five of the fifteen cabinet ministers who affixed their names to the new constitution of Japan were subsequently designated as purgees.[24]

Many critics of the purge have stressed the ineffectiveness of the program, citing examples of purgees continuing to exercise their influ-

[20] Sumimoto, *op. cit.*, pp. 120–133.

[21] For further details, cf. *infra*, pp. 68–69.

[22] Imperial Ordinance No. 1, January 4, 1947, Article III, paragraphs 4 and 5. *PRJ*, Vol. II, p. 501.

[23] *PRJ*, Vol. I, p. 24.

[24] The fifteen who signed the Constitution (asterisks indicate purgees) were: Prime Minister Yoshida Shigeru, Minister of State Shidehara Kijuro, Minister of Justice Kimura Tokutaro, *Minister of Home Affairs Omura Seiichi, Minister of Education Tanaka Kotaro, Minister of Agriculture and Forestry Wade Hiroo, Minister of State Saito Takao, Minister of Communications Hitotsumatsu Sadayoshi, Minister of Commerce and Industry Hoshijima Niro (Jiro), Minister of Welfare Kawai Yoshinari, *Minister of State Uehara Etsujiro, Minister of Transportation Hiratsuka Tsunejiro, *Minister of Finance Ishibashi Tanzan, *Minister of State Kanamori Tokujiro, and *Minister of State Zen Keinosuke.

ence subsequent to designation. If consideration is given to the power which purgees continued to exercise as prerogatives of their office at the ministerial and lower levels, it is true that influence exercised by other purgees outside the government pales considerably by comparison.

Supervision of Purgee Activities

As has been noted, to designate an individual as a purgee was one step in eliminating his influence and authority. Merely to designate some 200,000 individuals would not assure, however, that the power which they had wielded would be denied to them. Problems of enforcing their full retirement from public life were thorny. Placing them in jails, as had been contemplated in the initial postsurrender directives, was ruled out at the inception of the purge.[25] To incarcerate them would go counter to the SCAP enunciated policy that the purge was a preventive rather than a punitive measure. Claims that General MacArthur had tempered the justice of the program with mercy could not have been made.[26] Immense problems would have had to be faced in completely removing purgees from public life, for this would have necessitated concentration or relocation camp-type institutions to house 200,000 people. Hence with this alternative ruled out, both at the policy and at the practical level, two alternatives remained. One was to enlist the support of the Japanese people to dissociate themselves from purgees. To do so would have necessitated an extensive propaganda campaign designed to bring the aims of the purge to the people. However, administrators of the purge paid only minimal attention to publicity; a few press interviews and one radio program were the only efforts made.[27] The second alternative was to include specific types of proscribed activity in the law, specify restrictive sanctions, and provide for enforcement by a well-organized investigating agency. It is this last, possibly most difficult alternative, which the purge administrators adopted.

---

[25] Cf. *supra*, pp. 7–8.

[26] Whitney, *op. cit.*, pp. 282–283.

"... there were many Japanese who, while not being actual war criminals, shared some degree of contributing responsibility for the policies that led Japan into a war of conquest. It was MacArthur's belief that though such persons should be barred for a time from any positions of power or influence, they should NOT be deprived of their civil rights and property or imprisoned as their counterparts had been in Germany. MacArthur's basic directive from Washington indicated that he should take into custody and hold for trial such 'militarists and ultranationalists.' But he interpreted it liberally and tried, through nonpunitive methods, to permit a new leadership to arise in Japan, untainted by undesirable traits from the past."

The official history put it more succinctly. "The indisputable justice of the purge was to be tempered with mercy." "Removal of Ultranationalists," *PRJ*, Vol. I, p. 13.

[27] *PRJ*, Vol. I, pp. 38–39.

Neither SCAPIN 550 nor its initial Japanese legal counterpart[28] contained any specific prohibitions concerning the activities in which a purgee could not participate. During 1946, nothing legally prevented a purgee who had been removed from office from returning to it and continuing to provide his former subordinates with guidance. In practice, those in public life usually went to the purgee. One rather famous incident will illustrate this point. In the latter part of 1946, there were continuous rumors that the chief secretary of the first Yoshida cabinet, Hayashi Joji, was constantly conferring with the purged ex-leader of the Liberal party, Hatoyama Ichiro. So persistent did the rumors become that corrective action became necessary to avoid a conclusion by the general public (and the American press corps) that the purge was a complete mockery. No legal action could be taken against either Hayashi or Hatoyama, for neither had violated anything but the spirit of the purge. Hence another form of persuasion was employed. Hayashi was called to GHQ, seated in front of the assembled members of Government Section, and berated for one hour by the section chief, General Whitney.[29] This method achieved its purpose temporarily but was no real solution to the problem.

Diffusion of responsibility within SCAP complicated the problem of supervision during the first year of the purge. Two GHQ staff sections shared responsibility for the implementation of the purge during 1946. These were the Civil Intelligence Section, which was under the direction of the Assistant Chief of Staff G-2, General Willoughby, and the Government Section headed by General Whitney. Theoretically, the division of functions intended the latter to be the policy-making agency and the former to investigate compliance. A basic difference in the mandate of each section influenced the orientation which they brought to the purge. The mission of the Government Section was to institute basic governmental reforms. The mission of the Intelligence Section, on the other hand, was to bring to light any danger to the security of Allied (and particularly American) forces. Whereas the redirection (or reorientation, in words of the official history) of Japanese society motivated the former, issues of security were of primary concern to the latter. So long as the main threat to the Occupation was conceived as coming from the ultranationalist-militarist (political) Right, the missions of the two sections meshed. General Willoughby, as early as December, 1945, however, voiced concern over the possibly unsettling

[28] Imperial Ordinance No. 109, February 27, 1946.
[29] Personal knowledge, based on participation in the meeting.

repercussions that the purge could have on the Occupation's tranquillity.[30] This concern was subsequently translated into a fear of the primary danger as coming from the political Left. Hence he did not view the purge, which was denuding the political Right of leadership, with enthusiasm. Government Section, in subsequently directing the purge against the leadership of the Japan Communist party, could not be said to favor the Communists. However, it believed that the requirements of the Potsdam Declaration should be carried out in good faith.

Given this basic difference in orientation existing between the two sections, a reasonable question would be, why was the purge not made the responsibility of one or the other? The answer lies in the Occupation policy to work through the existing structure of the Japanese government. Government Section had supervisory powers, but did not have investigative facilities with which to check compliance. That was to be the function of the Civil Intelligence Section, which could employ counterintelligence agents. Theoretically, Government Section would be informed of instances of noncompliance by the Japanese government, when these instances came to the attention of the Intelligence Section. This, however, was not always done. Motivated by an outlook differing from that of the Potsdam Declaration, General Willoughby sought to discredit Government Section. If General Whitney and his assistants did not have the information necessary to enforce the purge, it could not be properly administered. If it were not, Government Section would lose face and Civil Intelligence Section would be provided with the mantle of authority in its stead. Government Section, however, won its battle and in February, 1947, was given sole jurisdiction over the purge.[31]

Settling the jurisdictional problem did not solve Government Section's need for information concerning the Japanese government compliance with the purge. For its partial solution, Government Section had to rely on investigative agencies in the Japanese government itself. This decision brought about no real solution; on the contrary, it caused problems more numerous and more complex than before.

The Special Investigation Bureau

The Japanese government ordinances expanding the purge rectified some of the glaring omissions in the 1946 ordinance. Instead of moral (and hence meaningless) prohibitions, they contained specific injunc-

[30] Cf. *supra*, p. 25.
[31] General Order No. 1, February 13, 1946. *PRJ*, Vol. II, p. 798.

tions against purgees' engaging in proscribed activities. These injunctions included such prohibitions for a purgee as: engaging in political activity,[32] continuing to exercise his influence in the business with which he had been formerly associated,[33] and engaging in any public information activities.[34] These injunctions were given teeth by a penal provision that provided a maximum sentence of three years imprisonment or a fine not to exceed 15,000 yen (in 1949 amended to 100,000 yen).[35]

To include articles in the law which would delimit the scope of activi-

---

[32] Imperial Ordinance No. 1, January 1947, *PRJ*, Vol. II, p. 502.

Article XI. Any person in the public service shall neither establish nor maintain, in connection with his handling of official affairs or political activities, the continuity of influence of a person falling under the Memorandum on behalf of the latter by receiving instruction, advice or compensation from or communicating in any means with the latter.

Any person in the public service, when prosecuted pertaining to violation of the provisions of the preceding paragraph, shall not, regardless of the provisions of other laws and ordinances, carry out his official activities. . . .

Article XII. Any person falling under the Memorandum shall not cause a person in the public service, *in connection with handling of official affairs or political activities* of the latter, to establish or maintain, on behalf of him, the continuity of his influence by giving instruction, advice, or compensation to or by communicating in any means with the latter (italics mine).

[33] *Ibid.*

Article XIII. Any person falling under the Memorandum shall neither make entry into nor retain or set up his dwelling or office in the place of business of the last position, designated as public office . . . , which he occupied subsequent to July 7, 1937, from which he retired or which he forfeited, or in the place of business of government entity, company or other organization of business in which he had held the position causing his designation falling under the Memorandum or the place in the same premises which is under the management of such organizations. However, the provisions above *shall not be applied to such entry as may be necessitated by his conduct of his private life or as to be established legally.* [This article is written as amended by Cabinet Order No. 288, December 27, 1948. *PRJ*, Vol. II, p. 546 (italics mine).]

[34] *Ibid.*, pp. 502–503.

Article XIV. Any person who falls under the Memorandum who holds any position in an executive, staff or other capacity, in addition to those designated as public office, in any newspaper company, magazine or other publishing company, broadcasting corporation, company producing motion pictures, or in any other media of mass communication shall retire therefrom without delay.

Any person who falls under the Memorandum shall be excluded from any position proscribed in the preceding paragraph.

Article XIV (2). Any person designated by the Prime Minister as falling under the Memorandum who holds any position in an executive, staff or other capacity, in addition to those designated as public office, of a company or financial institution succeeding those specifically designated by the Prime Minister, shall retire therefrom without delay. . . . (Article XIV (2) added to Imperial Ordinance No. 1 by Prime Minister's Office Ordinance No. 11, February 9, 1948. *PRJ*, Vol. II, p. 546.)

[35] *Ibid.*, Article XVI. Any person who comes under any one of the headings below shall be liable to penal servitude of imprisonment for not exceeding three years or to a fine of not exceeding 100,000 yen. . . .

(6) Any person who has violated the provisions of Article XI, paragraph 1, Articles XII, XIII, XIV or Article XIV (2). . . .

ties proscribed for purgees was one matter. To enforce them presented entirely different problems. Until the dissolution of the Home Ministry in December, 1947,[36] its investigation section was charged with enforcing these injunctions and with enforcing the directive dissolving secret and terroristic societies.[37] That Government Section was willing to rely on the Home Ministry, generally considered as having bureaucratic power, may be difficult to understand. However, we must not forget the fact that the other investigative agencies of the Japanese government—the Special Higher Police (*Tokko-ka*) and the gendarmerie (*kempeitai*)—had been dissolved.[38] The Home Ministry Investigation Bureau did not exactly pursue its assigned tasks with vim and vigor, nor could we reasonably have expected the dissolved investigative agencies to have done so. We are again faced with General MacArthur's fundamental policy that the Japanese government was to operate its reform programs independently of SCAP control.[39] Even with SCAP control, the dissension between the Government Section and the Civil Intelligence Section would have undermined surveillance. To expect Home Ministry bureaucrats to fill the breach gives further evidence of Occupation emphasis on the issuance of directives rather than on compliance with them.

With the dissolution of the Home Ministry, these responsibilities were shifted to the newly established Special Investigation Bureau of the attorney general's office.[40] For the first time since the promulgation of the purge, a Japanese agency existed which had as one of its principal functions the surveillance of purgees. Takiuchi Reisaku, its first chief, had spent several years in jail during the 1930's for a violation of the Peace Preservation Law and could be expected to bring the requisite philosophy to the operation of the bureau. During its infancy, the bureau labored against almost insurmountable odds. Office space seemed to be unavailable, and adequate funds could not be found to enlarge the staff. Takiuchi's subordinates, for the most part, came from the old Investigation Bureau of the Home Ministry where their duties had also consisted of helping counterintelligence agents of the Occupation

---

[36] Cf. "The National Executive," *PRJ*, Vol. I, pp. 135–138.

[37] SCAPIN 548, January 4, 1946.*PRJ*, Vol. II, pp. 479–481. Also cf. *supra*, pp. 17–18.

[38] SCAPIN 93, October 4, 1946. *PRJ*, Vol. II, pp. 463–465.

[39] To back up this policy, a Staff Memorandum directed that all requests for information concerning the purge should be referred to the Japanese government. This directive had been issued in response to meddling by Occupation officials, who on occasion had prejudiced the action of the Screening Committee. Staff Memorandum No. 2, January 21, 1946. *PRJ*, Vol. II, p. 490.

[40] "Law for the Establishment of the Attorney General's Office," Law No. 193, December 17, 1947, Article VI. *PRJ*, Vol. II, p. 1060.

keep track of Japanese Communists.[41] Theories supporting the impartiality of administrators just do not stand up under this kind of strain.

In spite of these handicaps, however, four cases involving illegal activities by purgees had been sent to the procurator's office for prosecution within the bureau's first two months of operation. Leaders of major importance were included, like Yamamoto Katsuichi and Kono Ichiro, both former Liberal party members of the House of Representatives. The Urawa District Court (Saitama prefecture) handed down a decision of "not guilty" in the case of Yamamoto.[42] Kono did not fare as well. The case against him rested principally on his having participated in electoral campaigns, subsequent to his designation as a purgee, by furnishing campaign funds to Miura Toranosuke and Isozaki Teiji, both subsequently successful as candidates for membership in the House of Representatives. He was sentenced to ten months in jail by the Tokyo District Court.[43]

Some cases, of course, never reached the courts. Numerous reports circulated, for example, concerning the varying activities engaged in by Hatoyama Ichiro—specifically, that Hatoyama had met with Liberal party Secretary General Ono Bamboku, and Progressive party Diet members Yamamoto Takeo and Oasa Tadao.[44] The meeting took place at an Atami hotel which was owned by a local Liberal party boss, Hatakeyama Tsurukichi. Shortly after this meeting, Yoshida Shigeru also journeyed to the same hotel for a meeting with Hatoyama. Witnesses were available to substantiate these facts. Concurrently rumors were circulating that a merger between the Liberal party and a section of the Democratic party was contemplated. (These rumors later became fact in the formation of the Democratic-Liberal party in the fall of 1948.) Let us suppose that an indictment based on these allegations against these politicians had been brought into court and accepted as evidence. The procurator would rest his case on the evidence, asserting that it was sufficient to prove that the individuals had violated the

[41] Personal interview with Takiuchi Reisaku, June 10, 1948.

[42] Saiko Saibansho Jimu-Sokyoku Keijikyoku (Supreme Court, General Affairs Bureau, Prosecution Section), *Keiji Saiban Shiryo Dai Sanjuhachi Go: Koshoku Tsuiho Kankei Jiken Hanketsu Shu* (*Criminal Courts Records No. 38: Collection of decisions of cases connected with the public office purge*) [hereafter *Keiji Saiban Shiryo*]. 1949, Vol. I, pp. 194–275.

[43] *Keiji Saiban Shiryo*, 1949, Vol. I, pp. 49–63.

[44] This information has been taken from a report prepared by the Chief of the Home Ministry Investigation Section, Nishimura Naomi, who shortly after submitting it lost his job owing to the dissolution of the Home Ministry. He subsequently joined the private secretariat of Yoshida Shigeru and is at present a Liberal-Democratic party member of the House of Representatives. *Shugiin Yoran*, *op. cit.*, p. 161.

injunctions in the ordinance pertaining to meetings between purgees and persons hold public office. However, the injunction prohibited such meetings only if they were concerned "with the handling of official affairs of political activities."[45] For all that any person not present at the meetings could know, Hatoyama *et al.* had discussed the finer points of the tea ceremony. No evidence could be assumed to be available that "political" subjects had entered into their conversation.[46]

The Special Investigation Bureau also investigated violations of two further injunctions. The first concerned checking questionnaires to determine whether or not the answers were complete and correct.[47] Hirano Rikizo, whom we met earlier, had omitted from his questionnaire certain facts relevant to the determination of his status. He had not mentioned his directorship in the Japan Farmers' Union in April, 1932, nor his membership on the central executive committee of the National Socialist party, nor his having been editor and publisher of the Imperial Way Society's organ *Kodo* (Imperial Way). Since these facts constituted much of the evidence supporting his designation as a purgee,[48] he was indicted in the Tokyo District Court. Found guilty by that court[49] and sentenced to ten months' imprisonment, Hirano appealed to the Tokyo Superior Court, which reversed the lower court's ruling.[50] Hirano's was one of the very small number of cases in which omission from the questionnaire or the inclusion of falsehoods was taken to court. (Hirano had described the objectives of the Imperial Way Society as the improvement of the social position of peasants.) In most instances, no legal action was taken; the Japanese administrators believed that the individual's designation as a purgee constituted sufficient punishment and loss of face.[51]

The second injunction tried to confront one of the most pervasive sociological realities of the Japanese nation: the family system. Because of its importance, the injunction will be quoted in full.

---

[45] Imperial Ordinance No. 1, January 4, 1947, Articles XI and XII. For full texts, cf. *supra*, footnote 32, p. 70.

[46] Except, of course, if the Special Investigation Bureau could utilize some of the more pernicious techniques of modern crime-detection such as the paraphernalia of wire-tappers.

[47] Imperial Ordinance No. 1, January 4, 1947, Article XVI (3), "Any person who has been asked for presentation of material or explanation of facts ... but failed to do so or presented false materials or explanations, or materials or explanations lacking full and complete disclosures on relevant or material matters, ..." *PRJ*, Vol. II, p. 503.

[48] Cf. *supra*, pp. 54–57.

[49] *Keiji Saiban Shiryo*, No. 38, 1949, Vol. I, pp. 35–43.

[50] *Keiji Saiban Shiryo*, No. 53, 1951, pp. 1–49.

[51] Private conversations with personnel of the Special Investigation Bureau.

Article X. Any person who is a relative within the third degree by blood, marriage or adoption of any person who falls under the Memorandum shall be ineligible for a period of ten years from the day of the designation to succeed or to be appointed to any position or positions in the public service from which the latter has been removed . . . and, further, to exercise any of the power of the latter. The provision of the preceding paragraph shall not be applied to any elective position in the public service.[52]

Before inclusion of this article, there was a noteworthy exchange of views between Premier Yoshida and General MacArthur. Yoshida wrote that to make all family members, to the third degree, suffer was archaic and "contrary to the prevailing sense of justice."[53] The premier could have mentioned also, but did not, that the new Civil Code revised the legal family relationships and thereby attempted to establish a framework within which the traditional family system (often characterized as "feudal" by Japanese sociologists) would disappear.[54] We can argue that the Occupation should have been consistent in its views and that the inclusion of this family article among the injunctions in the purge ordinances would undermine Japanese confidence in the family system envisaged in the amended Civil Code, and was inconsistent therewith. Furthermore, its inclusion was a tacit admission that the traditional family system could not be altered solely by law.

General MacArthur, in his reply to Yoshida's letter, reviewed the characteristics of the traditional family system. "Article 186 (1) of the Code of Criminal Procedure recognizes the right of relatives within this third degree to refuse to give testimony against an accused relative. This provision in itself would make it impossible as a practical matter to convict any relative of colluding to perpetuate influence. . . ."[55] Of greater importance to SCAP, however, was the intent of the provision as aiding in the achievement of the objectives of the purge.

---

[52] Imperial Ordinance No. 1, January 4, 1947, Article X. *PRJ,* Vol. II, p. 502.

[53] Letter from Prime Minister Yoshida to General MacArthur, December 21, 1946. *PRJ,* Vol. II, p. 499.

"I remember reading something about a law or practice in China centuries ago that when a man was found to have committed a grave offense, all his relatives used to be sentenced accordingly. But I think the modern conception of justice let go completely free all relatives of even a murderer. To declare anyone 'undesirable' even for a specific position and even for a period of ten years simply because his relative, within the third degree, has been declared 'undesirable' seems contrary to the prevailing sense of justice."

[54] The Civil Code of Japan as amended by Law No. 222, December 12, 1947, *passim. PRJ,* Vol. II, pp. 1216–1283. But, cf. particularly Book IV: "Relatives" (pp. 1261–1270), and Book V: "Succession" (pp. 1270–1283).

[55] Letter from General MacArthur to Prime Minister Yoshida, December 26, 1946. *PRJ,* Vol. II, p. 500.

Any realistic program for removing the influence of individuals purged from influential posts must meet effectively the vital and irrepressible issue of collusion.... It is self-evident that such influence would be continued if a father, son, uncle, or nephew, etc., succeeded to the power of a purged individual. The provision merely sets up mechanics which will give fair assurance that the purge will not become a mockery through the device of "dummies." It does strike at that dangerous concentration of economic and political power which resides in the traditional family system. . . . It will establish unequivocally the purpose of the Japanese people to entrust the future of the nation to a leadership, political and economic, which has not been an influential or controlling part of either the private socialism of concentrated economic power or the totalitarianism of an authoritarian government. Both endanger democratic government by affording exclusive opportunity to a favored few. The proposed family article by insuring the diffusion of power and responsibility would tend to achieve this purpose in a manner consistent with our established aims.[56]

The Occupation on the one hand was utilizing an explanation of the traditional Japanese family system to buttress a purge injunction, and on the other hand, it was attempting to reconstruct the family system by amending the Civil Code. We can view both efforts as complementary, that the purge injunction served to emphasize the cutting of familial ties. Or we can accept the legal view, namely, that these ties no longer existed, so that Article X was an anachronism. In spite of the controversy which surrounded this family article of the purge injunctions, its enforcement proved to be almost impossible. One roadblock lay in the second paragraph which exempted elective positions.[57] As a result, wives and other relatives of purged Diet members were free to run for the seats vacated by their husbands. (The influence of these replacements, however, was not excessive if viewed within the total context of the purge.) A second roadblock to full enforcement lay in the article's exemption from the penal provisions which covered the other injunctions.[58] This article was the first to be deleted from the purge ordinances.[59]

The task of enforcing these injunctions was no easy matter. Takiuchi and his staff struggled manfully to fulfill their mandate, but the assignment would have been well-nigh impossible under the best of circumstances. The injunctions were so complex and the line between legal and illegal activities in which purgees could engage was so indistinct

[56] *Ibid.*

[57] Cf. *supra*, p. 74.

[58] Imperial Ordinance No. 1, January 4, 1947, Article XVI, *PRJ*, Vol. II, pp. 503–504.

[59] Cabinet Order No. 220, June 18, 1951. *Official Gazette* No. 1567 (Eng. ed.), June 18, 1951, p. 5.

that one of the investigation bureau officials finally published a book setting forth these matters at greater length and with more clarity than a reading of the law itself would provide.[60]

Since 1948 (until October of that year it was under the directorship of Takiuchi Reisaku) the Special Investigation Bureau had undergone a metamorphosis.[61] It has the dubious distinction of having been the precursor of the Public Safety Investigation Agency charged with administering the "Subversive Activities Prevention Act."[62] What began as an agency to control the activities of purged militarists and ultranationalists ended up as the reincarnation, both in personnel and in policy, of the thought-control police.

Summary

To designate an individual as a purgee was a step, important in itself, in the process of eliminating the influence and authority of those who had misled the Japanese people. Merely to designate some 200,000 individuals would not assure, however, that the authority which they had wielded had been denied to them. The problem of how to enforce their removal was a thorny one. To place these people behind bars, as had been contemplated in the initial postsurrender directive, was ruled out at the inception of the purge program. The purgees, except those in the war criminal category, had not been accused of crimes. Furthermore, to incarcerate them would go counter to the stated policy that the purge was a preventive rather than a punitive measure. In retrospect it would seem obvious that specific sanctions should have been written into the law, to insure that purgees would not attempt to perpetuate their influence. Yet neither the purge directive nor its original Japanese legal counterpart contained such provisions. During 1946, a purgee could continue to exercise power with no fear of legal retribution. The purge extension ordinance of 1947 corrected this omission. To include

[60] Ueda Shunkichi and Takahashi Masumi, *Tsuihōsha no Undō no Genkai* (*Limits of Activities of Purgees*).

[61] In October, 1948, the second Yoshida Cabinet came into office. Takiuchi, who had made himself unpopular by the investigation of purged Liberal party politicians, came under relentless attack. Yoshida managed to force Takiuchi's resignation by telling General MacArthur that the reason for Takiuchi's indictment under the Peace Preservation Law had been his having made a financial contribution to the Japan Communist party. Takiuchi had reported this fact in his questionnaire and a full investigation into his political affiliation (Social Democratic party: right-wing) had been undertaken prior to his appointment. Takiuchi's replacement was a former thought procurator who had participated in the prosecution of the Sorge spy ring.

[62] Law No. 240 of 1952. For text in English, cf. *Contemporary Japan*, Vol. XXI, Nos. 4–6, 1952, pp. 328–337.

articles in a law delimiting the scope of activities which purgees could exercise was one matter. To enforce them presented entirely different problems. Occupation investigation facilities did not effectively coöperate in this effort. As a result, Japanese government agencies had to be called in to undertake the task of surveillance.

Occupation purge enforcers became impaled on the horns of a dilemma which compromised the effectiveness of the purge. On the one hand, the objective of the purge was to eliminate the influence and authority of Japan's erstwhile masters. This objective would be accomplished neither by designating them as purgees nor by excluding them from key positions, in view of the strong family ties and those existing between a leader and his followers (the *oyabun-kobun* relation). Only by tackling these relationships could the purge accomplish its aim. To do so would necessitate denying certain individual rights to purgees and, to a lesser extent, to their families. On the other hand, the Occupation was trying to inculcate respect for those individual freedoms deemed fundamental to any theory of liberal democracy. This was done by issuance of the civil liberties directive, by inducing amendments in the Civil Code, and by including a substantial list of civil rights in the new constitution.

Whatever one's position on this theoretical paradox, its existence points up the unpopularity of the purge. Had the Japanese people, through their representatives in the political parties, felt a deep resentment against their wartime masters, merely to designate them would have sufficed to diminish their power. Instead, an investigative organization was considered necessary, was established and given substantial power. Once this step was taken it could, and did, lead to the reëstablishment of an embryonic thought-control police. This step was considered necessary because none of the major political parties gave strong support to the program. The conservative Liberals and Democrats had every reason to view the purge with loathing since it deprived them of their leadership. The Social Democratic party balked at the prospect of creating a strong investigation bureau. Only the Japan Communist party (minimal in strength by comparison to the others) supported the program, but for reasons far removed from Occupation objectives. Its support quickly dissipated once the purge was turned against the party leadership in the summer of 1950.

Despite these handicaps, however, a substantial number of former leaders were designated as purgees and, within the limitations noted, were removed from exercising their authority and influence.

Chapter VII

IMPACT OF THE PURGE

Several factors affected the impact of the purge program on Japanese leadership and indirectly on the people of Japan. Most crucial of these was the timing of various phases of the purge: (1) the early return of purgees to public life made the task of assaying the influence of temporary removals and/or exclusions particularly difficult; (2) the purge criteria indicated the strong bias of the Occupation policy makers and inculcated this bias into the implementation of the purge. This seriously affected the kind of impact that the purge could make. However, substantial repercussions were felt among the ranks of Japanese leaders as a result of the program.

Timing of Phases

The timing of the various phases of the purge made its impact uneven during the years when it was operative. Its implementing phase reached the high-water mark in 1948. By May of that year the Japanese government had designated some 200,000 purgees.[1] Concurrently, their surveillance was in the hands of a fairly effective investigating agency.[2] Before 1948, the impact that the purge might have had was limited by the fact that the designation process had not yet been completed. As a result, potential purgees still held positions of trust in public life. Furthermore, control over the activities of those designated had been practically nonexistent. During 1946, when the purge might have had its greatest influence on every important category of Japanese leadership, only personnel in the national government were affected by it.[3] Subsequent to the summer of 1948, the purge became a holding operation.

The "reverse course"[4] which dominated the formulation of policy during the Occupation's later years (1948-1952), also influenced the implementation of the purge. Successive waves of appeals and rescinding of entire purge categories brought an ever-increasing group of

[1] "General Summary of Purge Statistics" (as of May 10, 1948). *PRJ*, Vol. II, p. 553. The total number of purgees was 201,815.

[2] Cf. *supra*, pp. 69–76.

[3] Cf. *supra*, chap. iii, *passim*.

[4] Idiomatic expression used by Japanese to indicate the switch in Occupation policy from having emphasized "reform" to emphasizing "recovery" in order that Japan might become a military and economic bulwark against Communist expansion in eastern Asia.

purgees back into public life. Their return is best illustrated by table 1. As a result of these reinstatements only 8,710 persons were still purgees by the effective date of the Peace Treaty.[5]

By contrast, in 1950 SCAP utilized the purge to remove from influence the leadership of the Japan Communist party.[6] (In addition, some 20,997 Communists and fellow travelers lost their jobs in government, information media, and private industry in the period 1949–1951.[7]) The Occupation objective, noted earlier,[8] that Japan emerge from the period

TABLE 1

REINSTATED CASES

Agency	Terms	Number of persons appealed	Number of persons reinstated
1st Appeals Board	Mar. 3, 1947–May 10, 1948	1,085	148
Application for administrative rescission of designation	June 24, 1948–Apr. 4, 1949	2,363	1,522
2nd Appeals Board	Feb. 8, 1949–Mar. 31, 1951	32,127	10,090
Depurge of young officers of army and navy	Oct. 31, 1951	..	3,250
Administrative depurge by categories	June 18, 1951–Nov. 6, 1951	..	177,261
3rd Appeals Board	Nov. 29, 1951–Apr. 28, 1952	9,943	9,306
Total		45,518	201,577

SOURCE: Statistics Bureau, Prime Minister's Office, 1952. (Separate copy, typed.)

of tutelage with a leadership of moderates, was compromised by the timing of the so-called "red purge," for the latter coincided with the release from designation of the political extreme Right.

Finally, the relatively short duration of time during which the purge

[5] Statistics Bureau, Prime Minister's Office, 1952 (separate copy, typed).

[6] Letter from General MacArthur to Yoshida June 6, 1950. Cf. *supra*, p. 9, for text of letter.

[7] Concurrent with the designation of Communist party leaders as purgees, the Japanese government, information media, and industry took informal steps to remove Communists and fellow travelers; 10,793 were removed from government posts in 1949. By October, 1950, 690 personnel of broadcasting, news agency and newspaper companies, had been dismissed, and 9,514 workers in private industry had lost their jobs, making a total of 20,997 dismissals. "Control of Anti-Democratic Elements," pp. 42–44. This program came to be known as the "Red Purge." Except for the designation of the party's Executive Committee and editorial staff of *Akahata*, the party organ, dismissals did not take place by means of designation under the purge.

[8] Cf. *supra*, chap. ii, *passim*.

was operative must be taken into consideration. General Whitney had stated in June, 1948, "Final action taken under the purge program is regarded to be of a permanent nature for which the Allied Powers will unquestionably hold future Japanese governments fully responsible."[9] This statement was in consonance with the clause of the Potsdam Declaration upon which rested the whole superstructure of the purge program.[10] A clause to this effect should have been included in the Peace

TABLE 2

PURGEES BY CATEGORIES

Category	Number	Per cent
Military elite	167,035	79.6
Bureaucratic elite	1,809	.9
Political elite	34,892	16.5
Ultranationalistic elite	3,438	1.6
Business elite	1,898	.9
Information Media elite	1,216	.5
Total	210,288	100.0

SOURCE: Statistics Bureau, Prime Minister's Office and chart in Kinoshita Hanji, *Purge Policy and After*, Tokyo: Nihon Taiheiyo Mondai Chosakai (Japan Institute of Pacific Relations), 1954, pp. 33–35

Treaty in order to have made effective the permanency of the purge. This, however, was not done.[11] As a result the Japanese government issued ordinances revoking the purge in its entirety, and these came into force the day after the Peace Treaty became official.[12]

[9] SCAP Press Release, June 22, 1948, as quoted in *PRJ*, Vol. I, p. 44.

[10] "There must be eliminated *for all time* the authority and influence of those who have deceived and misled the people of Japan" (italics mine). For full text of clause, cf. *PRJ*, Vol. II, p. 413.

[11] For text of Japanese Peace Treaty, cf. United States Department of State, *United States Treaties and Other International Agreements*, 1952, Vol. III, Part 3, "Multilateral Treaty of Peace with Japan." Washington, D.C., U. S. Government Printing Office, 1955, pp. 3169–3191. In a real sense the permanency of the purge was no longer at issue by the time the Peace Treaty came into effect; only 8,710 persons remained purged out of the total of 210,288 designated.

[12] Law 94. "Law for the Abolition of the Imperial Ordinance concerning the Exclusion, Retirement, etc., in Respect to Public Offices, etc." "Article I: The following Law and Ordinances shall be abolished: (1) . . . Imperial Ordinance No. 1 of 1947. . . . This law shall come into effect as from the day of the first coming into force of the Treaty of Peace. . . ." *Official Gazette* (Eng. ed.) No. 1822, April 21, 1952, pp. 9–10. Cabinet Order No. 117, "General Amnesty Order," "Article I: The persons who have committed the offenses mentioned below prior to April 28, 1952 . . . shall be pardoned: . . . (24) Offenses against the following laws, orders, and ordinances; (a) . . . Imperial Ordinance No. 1 of 1947. . . ." *Official Gazette*, Extra No. 43 (Eng. ed.), April 28, 1952, pp. 1–2.

Influence of the Criteria

Purgees fall into six categories of elites. These are the military, bureaucratic, political, ultranationalistic, business, and information media elites. The relative impact of the purge criteria can best be indicated by a summary of designations made in each of these categories. Basic policy emphasis on the military and ultranationalists as the groups most culpable for having deceived and misled the Japanese people is indicated in table 2.

Militarists

The military elite is by far the largest numerical group affected by the purge. Table 3 shows the categories and numbers included.

TABLE 3

The Military Elite

Category	Subtotal	Total
War criminals		3,422
Career military personnel		122,235
Army officers	53,854	
Navy officers	27,691	
Chokunin rank army civilians	62	
Chokunin rank navy civilians	109	
Military police (*Kempeitai*)	39,394	
Army special intelligence agents (*Tokumu kikan*)	1,055	
Navy special intelligence agents (*Tokumu bu*)	70	
Branch chiefs of the Imperial Ex-Serviceman's Association (*Zaigo Gunjin Kai*)		41,378
Total		167,035

Source: Statistics Bureau, Prime Minister's Office and chart in Kinoshita Hanji, *Purge Policy and After*, Tokyo: Nihon Taiheiyo Mondai Chosakai (Japan Institute of Pacific Relations), 1954, pp. 33–35.

The purge eliminated the military elite in its entirety from the ranks of Japanese leadership. It is possible that a few nonmilitary men are included in the group of war criminals listed in table 3. However, in order to avoid duplication the Japanese government listed war criminals under appropriate purge categories so far as possible.[13] Hence the number of nonmilitary personnel should be very small. Only officers were included among the career military personnel. Enlisted men were purged only if they had served in the gendarmerie or in special intelligence organs of the military services.

[13] "General Summary of Purge Statistics," *PRJ*, Vol. II, p. 553, footnote 1.

Bureaucrats

The purge removed a relatively small group from the ranks of the bureaucracy; nearly 100 military or ex-military personnel were designated for every bureaucrat purged. Few of the purge criteria were specifically aimed at eliminating members of the civil service. Criteria purging cabinet ministers and high public officials affected 145 members of the senior civil service; criteria concerning political police and "thought" procurators affected 356 individuals; and those criteria concerning governors of occupied territories purged 89.[14] The vast majority (1,219) of bureaucrats fell under the so-called *Butokukai* (Military Virtue Society) criteria. Considerable controversy surrounded the inclusion of the *Butokukai* in the purge criteria. The organization's officers were for the most part police officials in the Home Ministry. Criteria purging its officials were among the very few designed to remove lower-echelon civil bureaucrats, in particular police personnel. Out of the total of 1,809 bureaucrats purged, the *Butokukai* criteria accounted for 67 per cent.[15]

TABLE 4

Bureaucratic Elite

Bureaucrats	Number	Per cent
Number of bureaucrats screened	42,251	100.0
Number of bureaucrats purged	830	1.9
Shinnin[a] rank screened	87	100.0
Shinnin rank purged	42	48.3
Chokunin[b] rank screened	1,974	100.0
Chokunin rank purged	164	8.3
Sonin rank screened	40,190	100.0
Sonin rank purged	624	1.55

Source: Statistics based on information prepared by Statistics Bureau, Prime Minister's Office (private copy). These statistics include only those screened and not those who retired or resigned and subsequently were provisionally designated. Hence the discrepancy between the total number of bureaucrats purged (1,809) and the total number here given (830).

[a] *Shinnin* rank was held by ministers and privy councilors appointed by the Emperor.

[b] *Chokunin* rank was also by imperial appointment; it included vice-ministers and other senior civil servants.

[14] Kinoshita, *op. cit.*, pp. 33–35.

[15] For a more complete survey of the *Butokukai's* inclusion in the purge criteria and its results, cf. *PRJ*, Vol. I, pp. 67–72. In the statistics therein provided (at p. 72) the total given is 1,320 designated. At the time the statistics were prepared, a number of cases involving the consideration of counterevidence were pending before the Screening Committees. These account for the discrepancy.

Table 4 indicates the purge criteria's impact on the bureacracy. The statistics clarify the extremely limited impact of the purge criteria upon the top crust of the bureaucracy; 1 out of 2 *Shinnin* rank, not quite 1 out of every 10 of *Chokunin* rank, and only slightly more than 1 out of every 100 of *Sonin* rank bureaucrats were removed. Yet all three ranks included policy-making officials.[16] The purge left the bureaucracy almost unchanged in the composition of its personnel.

TABLE 5

PROGRESSIVE PARTY (KAISHIN TO)
(Including the Democratic Party, the People's Coöperative Party, the Coöperative Democratic Party and members drawn from the prewar *Minseito*, People's Political Party)

Year	Candidates for and members of House of Representatives	Candidates for and members of House of Councillors	Candidates and elected governors	Total
1946	5	..	..	5
1947	25	5	3	33
1948	167[a]	..	..	167[a]
1949	1	..	..	1
Purged after screening	31	5	3	39
Provisional designees	167[a]	5	3	167[a]
Total	198	5	3	206

SOURCE: Kinoshita Hanji, *Purge Policy and After*, p. 17.
[a] Candidates purged under the provisional designation program.

POLITICIANS

The impact of the purge on the political elite can best be seen by analyzing its effect on political party leadership. One category of purge criteria, that concerning the Imperial Rule societies, was the handle by which undesirable elements in the political elite were purged. Out of a total of 34,892 designated as purgees in this group, 34,396 had been national or prefectural officials of the Imperial Rule Assistance Association (*Taisei Yokusan Kai*) and its affiliates; 434 had been Diet members "recommended" to the voters by the Imperial Rule Assistance Political Society (*Taisei Yokusan Seiji Kai*) in the 1942 wartime elec-

[16] Cf. *supra*, pp. 62–64.

tion. The remainder (62) were leaders of the Communist party designated in 1950.[17]

Leadership of the Progressive party was the most seriously affected by the purge in its initial stage. This party had held a majority of the seats (274 out of 466) in the pre-1946 election Diet. Only 27 wartime Diet members who had joined the Progressive party upon the dissolution of the Imperial Rule Assistance Political Society (*Taisei Yokusan Seiji Kai*) remained unaffected by the initial purge order.[18] Subsequent thereto, the party's candidates for important elective positions fared as shown in table 5.

The Progressive party initially attempted to reconstitute itself on the basis of its local organizational structure, which remained intact until the extension of the purge to local government officers in 1947. With the extension of the purge, some of the party leaders recognized that the party would have to reorganize itself and redefine its policy orientation if it were to survive as a force in Japanese politics. Consequently, one faction made a valiant attempt to revitalize the party by adopting a less reactionary platform. It was partly successful in ousting the entrenched leadership of Shidehara Kijuro, and renamed the organization the Democratic party. It had to overcome the purge of four important reorganizers—Inukai Ken, Narahashi Wataru, Ishiguro Takeshige, and Chizaki Usaburo. The Central Screening Committee under the chairmanship of Matsushima had designated them within the three weeks just before the 1947 election.[19] The widely held contention that these removals were motivated by political considerations was supported by two principal lines of argument. First, Shidehara resented the revolt within the Progressive party against his leadership which had been headed by Ashida Hitoshi[20] and the four individuals named above. Also, Yoshida was anxious to see a union between the two conservative parties (Liberal and Democratic); he believed that it could more readily take place if Shidehara's leadership remained unchallenged. In 1948, Shidehara and his faction did join a partial amalgamation of conservative forces entitled the Democratic-Liberal party.[21]

---

[17] Kinoshita, *op. cit.*, pp. 33–35.

[18] *PRJ*, Vol. I, pp. 25–26.

[19] Cf. *supra*, p. 52.

[20] Cf. *infra*, pp. 95–96.

[21] For further details concerning these intra- and inter-party struggles, cf. "Political Parties," *PRJ*, Vol. I, pp. 348–352. Not to be confused with the Liberal-Democratic party which came into existence in November, 1955. This merger, led by Hatoyama Ichiro, was joined in by all conservative party members in the House of Representatives with the exception of Yoshida Shigeru and two of his followers, Hashimoto Tomisaburo and Sato Eisaku.

The Liberal party, conservative party colleague of the Progressive party, initially sustained less formidable blows. Of its 50 members in the lame-duck session held over from the wartime Diet, only 10 were purged.[22] The party lost 198 individuals destined for high office in the years 1946-1948.

Hatoyama's designation as a purgee on the very day that a letter to SCAP from Premier Shidehara recommended him as the next prime

TABLE 6

THE LIBERAL PARTY (JIYU TO)

(Including the Democratic-Liberal party, the Japan Liberal party, and the prewar *Rikken Seiyu-Kai* [Political Friends of Constitutionalism Society])

Year	Candidates for and members of House of Representatives	Candidates for and members of House of Councillors	Candidates and elected governors	Total
1946	4	..	..	4
1947	31	5	4	40
	153[a]	..	..	153[a]
1948	1	..	..	1
1949	..	..	..	..
Purged after screening	36	5	4	45
Provisional designees	153[a]	..	..	153[a]
Total	189	5	4	198

SOURCE: Kinoshita Hanji, *Purge Policy and After*, p. 16.
[a] Candidates purged under provisional designation program.

minister was the most substantial loss suffered by the Liberal party. This instance of the purge of one man[23] serves as an excellent example of the fact that the impact of the purge cannot be measured merely in numbers of individuals purged. The purge of a potential prime minister had far greater repercussions on politics than could the designation of thousands of Imperial Rule Society branch chiefs or the like. Yoshida Shigeru, upon whom Hatoyama conferred his mantle of leadership, regrouped Liberal party forces. He relied on a few old party bosses such as Ono Bamboku but depended most heavily on ex-bureau-

[22] *PRJ*, Vol. I, p. 26.

[23] Cf. *supra*, pp. 21–24, for reasons that Hatoyama was purged. In his account of the case, Mark Gayn (*Japan Diary*, pp. 161–164), implies that had it not been for pressure put to bear on SCAP by the foreign correspondents, Hatoyama would not have been purged.

crats to fill party ranks.[24] This was an astute move in terms of the purge, for the removal program did not cut too deeply into the ranks of Japan's professional officialdom.

What had been the career of Yoshida Shigeru, who replaced Hatoyama Ichiro? Yoshida, whose tenure as prime minister extended from April, 1946, through April, 1947, and from October, 1948, to April, 1952[25] (a total of 55 out of the Occupation's 80 months), had had a long and varied career.[26] He had been consul general in Mukden at the time of Marshal Chang Tso-lin's assassination. (No evidence has ever come to light indicating that he played a part in the Marshal's demise.) Yoshida had also been vice-minister of foreign affairs in the Tanaka Giichi cabinet which had followed a "strong" (euphemism for expansionist) policy vis-à-vis China. Hatoyama had served as chief cabinet secretary in this cabinet, and this service was among the reasons given for his purge.[27] Whether Yoshida should be included among those who had "played an active and predominant governmental part in the Japanese program of aggression"[28] was the subject of considerable controversy. Yoshida was saved from the purge by the fact of his participation in the 1945 spring "peace plot" for which pains he was temporarily incarcerated by the gendarmerie (*kempeitai*). This is the only major difference between the careers of Yoshida and Hatoyama, with the exception that the former was a career bureaucrat and the latter a parliamentarian.

Of the major political parties, the Social Democratic party was least affected by the purge. To be sure, it sustained a heavy loss in experienced leadership percentage-wise, for 10 of its 17 representatives in the wartime Diet were disqualified from public office.[29] In comparison to the conservative parties, which lost 206 and 198 major leaders respectively in the 1946–1949 period, the Socialists were decreased by

[24] In the April, 1946, election, 2.7 per cent of Liberal party adherents in the House of Representatives were ex-bureaucrats. By the April, 1947, election, the percentage had increased to 12.1 per cent; in January, 1949, it was 18.2 per cent; and in the June, 1950, House of Councilors election 19.5 per cent of the Liberal party members were ex-bureaucrats. Oka Yoshisato, *Pattern of Power in Japanese Democracy*, Tokyo: Nihon Taiheiyo Mondai Chosakai (Japan Institute of Pacific Relations), 1954, p. 8.

[25] In actuality his premiership extended to December, 1955, when Hatoyama finally managed to wrest control away from Yoshida. The April, 1952, date is used because the Peace Treaty ending the Occupation came into effect on the 28th.

[26] Information is based on Yoshida Shigeru's questionnaire.

[27] Cf. *supra*, p. 22.

[28] SCAPIN 550, Appendix A, Category G, paragraph 3. *PRJ*, Vol. II, p. 485.

[29] *PRJ*, Vol. I, pp. 26–27.

only 34 individuals as is shown by table 7. The more limited impact of the purge on the Social Democratic party is readily understandable in view of the emphases of the purge criteria. The majority of the Social Democrats had either been in prison or been *persona non grata* during the militarist era. Hence, few had held positions or participated in activities which would make them subject to the purge criteria. In fact, if any one political group gained by the purge, it was the Social Democratic party. From a wartime representation of 17 in the House

TABLE 7

THE SOCIAL DEMOCRATIC PARTY (SHAKAI TO)
(Including the prewar Socialist Mass Party, Shakai Taishu To)

Year	Candidates for and members of House of Representatives	Candidates for and members of House of Councilors	Candidates and elected governors	Total
1946	3	..	..	3
1947	16	3	5	24
	4[a]	..	..	4[a]
1948	1[b]	..	..	1
1949	2[c]	..	..	2
Purged by screening	22	3	5	30
Provisional designees	4	..	..	4
Total	26	3	5	34

SOURCE: Kinoshita Hanji, *Purge Policy and After*, p. 17.
[a] Candidates purged under the provisional designation program.
[b] Hirano Rikizo.
[c] Matsumoto Jiichiro and Tanaka Shogetsu.

of Representatives (and a prewar high of 36), the party won 96 seats in the 1946 election and 144 seats in 1947.[30]

Until the summer of 1950, the Communist party leadership did not suffer any losses under the purge. Removals up to that time were militarists and ultranationalists, and during the wartime period Japanese Communists had been in prison or in exile. In June, 1950, however, the Communist party leadership felt the full weight of the purge. As a result of these removals, in addition to other complex factors, the

[30] Jichicho Senkyobu (Autonomy Agency Election Bureau), *Shugiin Giin Sosenkyo Kekka Shirabe* (*Investigation of House of Representatives General Election Results*) (hereafter, *Kekka Shirabe*) 1953, p. 10.

party lost all of its central committee[31] and 15 out of its total Diet membership of 37.[32] As yet the party has not recovered from these losses.[33]

Impact of the purge on the political elite, as represented by candidates for the national Diet, was substantial. In the 1947 election, how-

TABLE 8

THE JAPAN COMMUNIST PARTY (NIPPON KYOSAN TO)

Year	Candidates for and members of House of Representatives	Candidates for and members of House of Councilors	Others[a]	Total
1950	9	1	33	43
1951	4	1	14	19
Total	13	2	47	62

SOURCE: Kinoshita Hanji, *Purge Policy and After*, p. 32.
[a] Central Committee members not in Diet, Editorial Staff of *Akahata* (Red Flag), the party organ, and other Communist publications, and leaders of Communist organizations such as the League of Korean Residents in Japan.

TABLE 9

MINOR PARTY AND INDEPENDENT CANDIDATES

Year	Candidates for and members of House of Representatives	Candidates for and members of House of Councilors	Candidates and elected governors	Total
1946	1	..	..	1
1947	78	34	14	126
	126[a]	..	..	126[a]
1948	..	1	..	1
1949	1	..	..	1
Purged by screening	80	35	14	129
Provisional designees	126[a]	..	..	126[a]
Total	206	35	14	255

SOURCE: Kinoshita Hanji, *Purge Policy and After*, p. 18. (Chart does not include Communist Party which, though minor, has been treated separately.)
[a] Candidates purged under provisional designation program.

[31] "Control of Anti-Democratic Elements," pp. 36–41.

[32] *Kekka Shirabe*, 1953, pp. 10, 22, and Kinoshita, *op. cit.*, p. 32. (Of the thirty-seven Diet members, thirty-five were in the House of Representatives and two were in the House of Councilors.)

[33] In the October, 1952 election, the party won no seats in the House of Representatives; in the April, 1953 election it managed to win one seat; and in the February, 1955 election it won two seats. *Kekka Shirabe*, 1949, p. 10, and 1955, p. 9. (To be sure, other factors than the purge played a role in the loss of power by the Communist party.)

ever, two factors militated against the purge's encouraging the rise of a new leadership. First, the purge had not as yet touched the source of conservative party funds, namely, big business interests. Also, the conservative parties had on their side tradition and a vast network of local organizations manned by individuals similar in outlook to those purged. More than removing some members of the prewar and wartime political elite was necessary to equalize the contest between the established parties and those which became influential only during the postwar period.

TABLE 10

APRIL 1947 ELECTION

Party affiliation	Number of candidates[a] ( ) = elected		Candidates purged[b] ( ) provisionally designated[c]	
	House of Rep.	House of C.	House of Rep.	House of C.
Liberal	326 (131)	72 (38)	31 (153)	5
Democratic	350 (121)	54 (28)	25 (167)	5
(Progressive) Socialist	289 (143)	99 (47)	16 (4)	3
Communist	120 (4)	40 (4)	.. ..	..
Minor and independent	505 (67)	312 (132)	60 (120)	29
Total	1,590 (466)	577 (250)	132 (444)	42

[a] Kekka Shirabe, 1953, cf. p. 10.
[b] Kinoshita Hanji, *Purge Policy and After*, cf. pp. 16–18.
[c] Do not appear in total number of candidates.

In addition, minor party and independent candidates were purged (cf. table 9).

Hence, during the period 1946–1949, 692 successful and unsuccessful candidates for important elective positions were barred or removed from the posts they had been seeking or had attained. This number becomes more meaningful if reference is made to the total number of candidates running for the House of Representatives and House of Councilors. The election of April, 1947, will be taken as a case study (table 10).

However, within the conservative parties, certain changes in leadership did take place. How much of this change is directly attributable to the purge is open to question. The fact remains that it was because of Hatoyama's purge that Yoshida became prime minister. Neither differed on fundamentals to be sure; Hatoyama would have sought another replacement if they had. Nonetheless, whereas Hatoyama had been a parliamentarian, Yoshida had been a bureaucrat in the prewar era. Furthermore, Yoshida relied heavily on the ranks of professional officialdom to furnish Liberal party candidates, thereby channeling the search for new leadership into a source which was different from the parliamentarians who had supported Hatoyama. The latter's absence from the overt political scene for nearly six years and his acquisition of the premiership some eight years and a half after being initially considered for it, thus came at a crucial time. Not he, but Yoshida set the dominant tone of conservative party policies. This substitution, a direct result of the purge, made more difficult the continuation of a direct line between prewar and postwar leadership among the conservatives. Hence, though the purge did not play as significant a role as it might have in changing the personnel and outlook of the political elite of Japan as a whole, it did contribute to the rise of a different leadership in the conservative parties.

Ultranationalists

Professional ultranationalists, as a group, were among the most severely hit by the purge. Not only were they excluded from positions of influence, but their organizations were dissolved as well.[34] Although the number of ultranationalists designated as purgees represented only a small proportion (1.6 per cent) of the total number of purgees, the vast majority of these extremist leaders was included. In addition to all officers of the societies named, influential members were affected.[35] Only in the military elite did the purge cut as deeply.

Action taken against ultranationalists differed in one important respect from that taken against the other elites. Whereas the purge criteria, once established, remained constant, investigating agency surveillance periodically expanded the list of organizations to be dissolved. Concurrent with their dissolution, the organizations were added to the purge criteria. At the end of 1947, subsequent to which the other purge criteria remained frozen, the purge ordinance listed one hundred and twenty organizations of which the key personnel would be automatically subject to the purge. In 1948, thirty-six organizations were added to the list; in 1949, twenty more; in 1950, another thirty-three; and in 1951, an additional nine societies were dissolved and made part of the

[34] "Dissolution of Ultranationalistic Societies," *PRJ*, Vol. I, pp. 73–81. The property of the dissolved organizations was impounded by the government. Included for dissolution were a total of 227 societies during the 1946–1951 period. Kinoshita, *op. cit.*, pp. 21–22. (The total given by Kinoshita is incorrect on the basis of figures included in his chart.)

[35] Cabinet and Home Ministry Ordinance No. 1, January 4, 1947, Appendix I, paragraph 3. *PRJ*, Vol. II, pp. 410–511.

list.[36] Not all these associations were what might be termed ultranationalist in character. Five, in fact, were Communist or extreme leftist organizations.[37] Actions taken against these were tied to the dissolution and purge directives by both Occupation and Japanese government administrators on the basis that both types of groups were extremist and used terrorist tactics to achieve their policy aims. "The Supreme Commander will not permit any group in Japan, whatever its name or political affiliation, to incite violence and disrespect for Occupation directives or Japanese law. As long as the Occupation lasts, he will exact obedience to his orders and respect for the processes of representative government in all political activity. Be yourself warned and caution your fellows."[38] The clarity of this statement obscures the fact that it marked the shift in purge policy from emphasis on extreme right- to emphasis on extreme left-wing organizations.

Economic Personnel

An eminent American businessman has commented that "because of the purge [Japanese economic enterprises have] been stripped of older men of ability and experience. Japanese banks are being run by former cashiers and assistant vice-presidents while business concerns are being directed by former bank managers and clerks."[39] Official statistics inform us that the economic purge initially removed 1,973 out of a total talent pool numbering 8,309.[40] If these statistics are taken at their face value it would appear that the purge had deprived Japan of nearly one out of every four trained leaders. Without further amplification, they would certainly support his viewpoint.

---

[36] Kinoshita, *op. cit.*, p. 22.

[37] The League of Korean Residents in Japan (Zai *Nippon Chosenjin Remmei*) and three of its affiliates of whose reputed membership of 300,000, thirty-six were designated as purgees; the Tokyo Metropolis Shinjuku Committee of the Japan Communist party; the Greater Japan Printing Call (*Dai Nippon Insatsu Saibo*); and the Toho Cinema Studio cell of the Japan Communist party; and the National Liaison Council of Labor Unions (*Zenkoku Rodo Kumiai Renraku Kyogikai: Zenroren*). "Control of Anti-Democratic Elements," pp. 38–40.

[38] Statement made by General Whitney to Communist party member of the House of Representatives, Sunama Ichiro, as quoted in "Control of Anti-Democratic Elements," p. 34.

[39] James Lee Kauffmann, "Report of Conditions in Japan." Mr. Kauffmann was a member of the Strike Mission sent to Japan to prepare a report on Japan's industrial potential.

[40] This total 1,973 (*PRJ*, Vol. II, p. 558) differs slightly from that given by Kinoshita (1,898, cf. *supra*, table 2). I believe the difference can be explained in that Kinoshita's slightly smaller total is based on total remaining purged on the eve of the Peace Treaty plus total economic personnel already then reinstated. Among reinstatees, it is entirely possible that a few were listed under other categories. In any case, the variation is sufficiently minor not to change the conclusions which can be drawn on the basis of these statistics.

TABLE 11

THE ECONOMIC ELITE (AS OF MAY 10, 1948)

Category	Total personnel[a] affected	Personnel purged		
		By prov. desig.[b]	By screen.[c]	Total
Category V[d] (E of SCAPIN 550):				
(Officers of financial and development organizations involved in Japanese expansion)	452	391	42	433
Category VII[e] (G of SCAPIN 550):				
Paragraph O[f] (special companies, corporations, special banks, and other companies in which the government or other organizations mentioned above is the largest stockholder)	2,855	...	99	99
Paragraph 7[g] (companies or other organizations to be designed by the Temporary Supply and Demand Adjustment Law and those which are reorganizations of *Tosei Kai* Control Associations, *Tosei Kaisha* Control Companies, and *Tosei Kumiai* Control Guilds, established after Sept. 2, 1945)	843	...	41	41
Paragraph 8[h] (organizations established by special legislation, or subsidized by the government and other organizations serving for the public benefits corresponding to the above)	911	...	60	60
Paragraph 11[i] (influential companies, financial institutions, and other economic organizations):				
In Japan	2,451	666	332	998
Outside Japan	361	248	73	321
Paragraph 12[j] (influential companies, et cetera, other than listed in Par. 11)	436	...	21	21
Total	8,309	1,305	668	1,973[k]

SOURCE: *PRJ*, Vol. II, pp. 514–516; 529–531; 538–543; 553; 558–564.

[a] Total personnel screened plus total personnel purged (by screening and provisional designation) = "Total Personnel Affected." *PRJ*, Vol. II, pp. 558–560; 562–564.

[b] *PRJ*, Vol. II, pp. 562–564.

[c] *PRJ*, Vol. II, pp. 558–560.

[d] *PRJ*, Vol. II, pp. 514–515.

[e] *PRJ*, Vol. II, p. 516.

[f] *PRJ*, Vol. II, p. 529.

[g] *PRJ*, Vol. II, pp. 529–530.

[h] *PRJ*, Vol. II, pp. 530–531.

[i] *PRJ*, Vol. II, pp. 538–542.

[j] *PRJ*, Vol. II, pp. 542–543.

[k] This total (1,973) is slightly larger than the total (1,966 = Cat. E 431 and Cat. G a Economic 1,535) given in "General Summary of Purge Statistics," *PRJ*, Vol. II, p. 553, as two reinstatees in Cat. E and five in Cat. G, or a total of seven (1,966 + 7 = 1,973), had not been subtracted in the more detailed statistics. (*PRJ*, Vol. II, pp. 558–560; 562–564).

In order to provide a clearer indication of the impact of the purge on this category, several other factors should be noted. Included in the total number of personnel which constitute human resources of talent in the economic activity of Japan are officials from government corporations, from companies in which the government had a controlling interest, and from government economic control agencies, not only officials of private economic enterprises. Incidence of removals and exclusions is indicated in table 11. In private economic enterprises[41] only 468 out of a total of 2,395[42] business, financial, and industrial leaders were designated after screening. On the basis of this statistical evidence it is fallacious to believe that the purge substantially altered the composition of Japan's leadership in these fields of endeavor. True, fulfilling one of the objectives of the purge, some of the most able and capable leaders were removed because, "It was these very persons, born and bred as feudalistic overlords, who held the lives and destiny of the majority of Japan's people in virtual slavery, and who, working in closest affiliation with its military, geared the country with both the tools and the will to wage aggressive war. . . . Those are the persons who, under the purge, are to be removed from influencing the course of Japan's future economy."[43]

Certain other factors, in addition to these statistics, support the viewpoint that the purge was not entirely effective in altering Japan's business leadership. Nearly a year had elapsed between publication of the plan for extending the purge into economic enterprises and its actual implementation.[44] During the interim, potential purgees insured that their replacements would not alter corporation policies. Moreover, the economic purge, as has been noted, applied only to a limited number of enterprises. Hence purgees were free to take positions of leadership in many economic enterprises not specifically covered in the purge ordinance. Also, problems of surveillance made it virtually impossible to check on the continuity of influence exercised by purgees over the policies of companies from which they had been legally removed. Finally, the bulk of economic purgees remained removed for

---

[41] As represented by Categories V and VII, paragraphs 11a, b, and 12 on the preceding chart.

[42] Provisional designees are not included in either figure.

[43] General MacArthur's "Comment" on *Newsweek* article, entitled "Behind the Japanese Purge—American Military Rivalries," *PRJ*, Vol. II, p. 549.

[44] *PRJ*, Vol. I, pp. 46–57. The plan was published in November, 1946. Designations began in April, 1947, but did not really get under way until September of that year. The period could be considered as being in excess of eighteen months if the issuance of SCAPIN 550, January 4, 1946, is taken as the starting point.

a comparatively short period of time. By December, 1950, only 1,311[45] individuals remained designated (in contrast to the original 1,973), and by April, 1952 (on the eve of the Peace Treaty) all but 12[46] had had their designations removed and were free to return to public life.[47] All these factors lead to the conclusion that the purge was, at best, only temporarily and partly effective in changing economic leadership of Japan.[48]

TABLE 12

INFORMATION MEDIA ELITE

Category	No. of institutions[a]	Number of personnel			Number purged		Tota
		Screened[b]	Under prov. designation[c]	Total	After screening[b]	After prov. desig.[c]	
Newspaper and news agencies	218	595	276	871	120	256	376
Book and mag. publishers	303	640	255	895	62	213	275
Motion-picture theatrical cos.	18	73	28	101	22	28	50
Broadcasting corporations	6	20	15	35	5	15	20
Gov. inf. control agencies	5	..	62	62	..	59	59
Writers	..	..	331	331	..	286	286
Total	605	1,328	967	2,295	209	857	1,066

[a] Total number of institutions = number of institutions listed under Cabinet and Home Ministry Ordinance No. 1, January 4, 1947. Category VII "Remarks," paragraph 5 d i (a), (b), (c), (d), subparagraphs (1), (2), (3), (4), (5), *PRJ*, Vol. II, pp. 521-525.
[b] *PRJ*, Vol. II, p. 560.
[c] *PRJ*, Vol. II, p. 564.

INFORMATION MEDIA PERSONNEL

The public information media purge would seem to have been among the most stringent of the leadership removals effectuated by the purge program. At first glance, statistics inform us that of the 2,295[49] per-

[45] "Summary of Purge Statistics," as of December 31, 1950, in "Control of Anti-Democratic Elements," p. 18.
[46] Kinoshita, *op. cit.*, pp. 34–35.
[47] By comparison, the December, 1950 statistics in "Control of Anti-Democratic Elements," (p. 18) lists 112,792 "militarists" still designated, and Kinoshita, *op. cit.*, p. 33, lists 7,892 in that category not "unpurged" on the eve of the Peace Treaty.
[48] The purge, however, was not the only program which played a role in the Occupation's attempt to introduce changes in the leadership and structure of Japan's economy. For these, cf. T. A. Bisson, *Zaibatsu Dissolution in Japan, passim.*
[49] This number is based on the following statistics: 1,328 information media officials who were screened (*PRJ*, Vol. II, p. 560), plus 967 information media initially provisionally designated (*PRJ*, Vol. II, p. 564) = 2,295 total personnel considered as of May 10, 1948.

sonnel in this field of activity, whose careers came under the scrutiny of the purgers, 1,066 were removed[50] or (in case they had resigned before screening) were barred from their chosen profession.

As indicated by table 12, the vast majority of persons affected by the information media purge had resigned from their positions before screening. That is to say, only 209 out of 1,328 persons screened were purged. The other 857 purgees came from the ranks of provisional designees, which included 59 officials from government control agencies and 286 independent publicists. Furthermore, in the 596 private information concerns,[51] only 701 officials were purged. Thus, on the average, a loss of slightly more than 1 official was sustained by each company.

The limited impact of the public information purge criteria is best illustrated by a particular case. Ashida Hitoshi served as prime minister of the Japanese government from March to October, 1948. Of the four postsurrender premiers (Shidehara Kijuro, Yoshida Shigeru, and Katayama Tetsu, were the other three), Ashida's eligibility to hold public office was the one most seriously questioned under the purge criteria. Two aspects of his career were considered—primarily, his service as president of the *Japan Times and Mail* from 1933 to January, 1940 (which period partly included that deemed critical under the information purge: July, 1937, to December, 1941), and also the editorial policies pursued by the *Japan Times and Mail* over which he had some control. Of the first, or service aspect, the following was said:

> Review of the *Japan Times and Mail* between July, 1937, and January, 1940 reveals that Ashida Hitoshi is subject to removal from public office and exclusion from government service as an undesirable person under the provisions of paragraph 5, subparagraph "d," Interpretation of Category "G" by the JG [Japanese Government]. However much or however little the Foreign Office imposed its views upon the *Times and Mail*, Ashida as principal official of that newspaper must bear partial

[50] This number is based on the following statistics: 209 purged after screening (*PRJ*, Vol. II, p. 560), plus 857 purged after provisional designation (*PRJ*, Vol. II, p. 564), = 1,066 total remaining purged after screening or provisional designation as of May 10, 1948. The total (1,066) is slightly smaller than that total (1,216) given by Kinoshita whose totals are utilized in table 2, *supra*, p. 80. Several factors explain the difference. First, the public information media purge was the last to be implemented so that it had not been completed by May 10, 1948, when the *PRJ* statistics were prepared. Secondly, as a result of this delay, it is very likely that several purgees were added to the public information media category subsequent to May 10, 1948. The difference between the two figures is so negligible, however, that conclusions based on one or the other set would not differ. *PRJ* statistics are utilized for detailed breakdown as they are more complete than those of Kinoshita.

[51] That is, exclusive of the six broadcasting corporations and five governmental control agencies.

or full responsibility for an editorial policy which consistently and enthusiastically supported the government's program of naked aggression and ruthless exploitation in Asia, assumed a bellicose and threatening attitude toward the Western powers, dutifully repeated the distortions and falsehoods of Nazi propagandists and by glorifying militarism assisted in the creation of a war psychology among its readers.[52]

These allegations are substantiated at great length in the memorandum from which the above quotation was taken. Were this insufficient, Ashida could also have been designated as a man of letters who "advocated aggression or military nationalism, or actively contributed to such propaganda, or who through his political or philosophical doctrine laid down an ideological basis for the policies for the Greater East Asia, or New Order in East Asia or policies of a similar nature, or the Manchurian Incident, the China Incident, or the Pacific War."[53] Neither the information media criteria nor the more general criterion concerning a man of letters was applied. How did Ashida escape designation? The answer to this question has been given, in part, in an earlier section of this study.[54] The public information media subcommittee reasoned as follows: the *Japan Times and Mail* was published in English and its circulation was limited. Its influence on the Japanese people, consequently, was insignificant in comparison to the Japanese language press. Another set of circumstances is worth noting, also. Ashida had proved himself during the Occupation's first twenty months as one of the leaders in the less reactionary wing of the Progressive party. He was among those who were attempting to change the leadership of that party to form the Democratic party. His removal[55] after the screening committee's designation of fellow Progressives Chizaki, Inukai, Ishiguro, and Narashashi[56] probably would have doomed the efforts of that group to revitalize the party.

This case further illustrates two factors which have been referred to at various points. Numbers alone do not necessarily give an accurate indication of the impact that removal of certain leaders might have. And even the Occupation was willing, on occasion, to give primary consideration to the political situation rather than to enforce rigidly the purge criteria.

---

[52] Memorandum for the Chief, Government Section, May 30, 1947.

[53] Cabinet and Home Ministry Ordinance No. 1, January 4, 1947, Appendix I, Article VII, "Remarks," paragraph 5 c (1). *PRJ,* Vol. II, p. 518.

[54] Cf. *supra,* p. 39.

[55] The Japanese Screening Committee had passed Ashida, in large measure because of the status assigned to the *Japan Times and Mail* which rendered its officials only screenable but not purgeable. A further factor that may have influenced the Committee was that Ashida, aside from his newspaper presidency, had been and subsequently again became, a career bureaucrat in the Foreign Office.

[56] Cf. *supra,* p. 52.

Summary

Results of designating some 200,000 purgees clearly reflect the assumption by the policy planners and purge criteria formulators that the military and the ultranationalists had borne virtually all responsibility for having misled the people of Japan. Militarists, ultranationalists, and the political supporters of the wartime government, as exemplified by officials in the Imperial Rule societies, constituted the vast preponderance of purgees. These three groups accounted for more than 97 per cent of the total number of purgees. Conversely, not quite 2½ per cent of the purgees came from the ranks of the bureaucrats—the business, financial, and industrial leaders and information media personnel. Thus, the purge can be considered a success in having denuded Japan of her military and ultranationalist leaders and politically motivated emperor-worshipers for the period during which it was operative. In so doing, the purge contributed to the pacifistic and neutralist policy orientations now held by many Japanese.

Numbers alone do not reflect the impact of removals. Hatoyama's purge had far greater repercussions on national politics than did the removal of scores of younger career military personnel, branch chiefs of the Imperial Rule societies, and ex-servicemen's association. Even at the highest political level removals were not consistent. Only Shidehara and Katayama, who between them held the office of prime minister for eighteen of the Occupation's eighty months, did not have a shadow cast over their background by the purge criteria. Both Yoshida and Ashida, who were Japan's premiers for the balance of the period of direct foreign tutelage, were certainly borderline cases in terms of their eligibility to hold public office as defined in the purge ordinances.

Timing of removals from and return to public life of purgees also played a role in the kind of impact the purge could have on changing the leadership of Japan. First of all, those who were purged remained in that status for a comparatively short period of time. Thus whatever impact the removals might have had was temporary. Furthermore, the designation process itself took nearly two years and a half. An excessively long period was required to determine who the undesirables actually were; and that, after all, was to be only the beginning of the journey toward complete removal of their authority and influence. By the time designations had been made, SCAP was on the point of turning its back on reform. And finally, the gradually accelerating program of reinstating purgees coincided with the purge of Communists, which brought about a reorientation of the purge program from one extreme of the political spectrum to the other.

The kind of political leadership which SCAP desired for the Japanese people was throughout the basic issue in the removals. Initially, the program was clearly designed as a preventive measure, to remove militarists and ultranationalists from a possible role in Japanese leadership; the criteria and results achieved reflected this objective. In the subsequent phase of the program the objective was more positive in that the process of removals was intended to aid in bringing forth leaders who would bring the Japanese people onto the "paths of freedom and democracy." In the end SCAP refined this objective to include only leaders who were willing to work within a parliamentary framework. This shift was especially directed against those whose policy included willingness to employ terrorist tactics for the achievement of their aims. SCAP attempted to aid in strengthening the parliamentary process and the leaders supporting it by blocking at first the rightist nationalists and later the leftists. So long as it remained operative, then, the final objective of the purge was to encourage leaders who were oriented toward the Western world in general, and the United States in particular, to obtain positions of power in the Japanese government.

CHAPTER VIII

CONCLUSION

THE PURGE was an unprecedented experiment to change the leadership of a nation by peaceful means. By mid-1948, more than 200,000 individual leaders of Japan had been either removed or barred from public office. This in itself represented a substantial achievement, especially if it is considered that it had been accomplished without bloodshed. The reader is asked to remember these achievements, because the problems faced in effectuating these removals and the shortcomings of the program have been stressed in the preceding pages; these have been emphasized in the hope that knowledge of past errors will lead to their nonrepetition in the implementation of a similar program at some future time.

The "reverse course" of Occupation policy was probably the major factor undermining the success of the purge. Owing, in large part, to a major shift in world conditions, this factor was not inherent in the purge. It had, however, several repercussions on the program. The shortness of time that purgees remained out of office could be traced in large measure to the reverse course in policy. Most purgees remained in their political outcast status for less than five years, in contrast to the objective of the Potsdam Declaration that the removals should be "for all time." Even if many purgees had been reinstated because their appeals were accepted, the total impact of the purge could well have been greater had the whole program not been subject to complete revocation once the Peace Treaty came into force.

The shift in Occupation policy also had the ultimate effect of switching the objective of the purge from removing militarists and ultranationalists to removing Communists and their sympathizers. This reverse course was further emphasized in that the "red purge" coincided with the depurge of militarists and ultranationalists. This coincidence of timing had the effect of giving the impression that the Occupation was no longer concerned about the democratization process in Japan, but thought only of the international cold war. As will be noted below, other factors besides the over-all shift in Occupation policy played a role in this reversal of purge policy. Whatever causal factors induced the shift, however, the fact that a reverse course in over-all Occupation policy was embarked upon seriously undermined whatever influence the purge might have had.

Reversal of purge policy can be traced most clearly in noting the shifts which took place in the objectives of the purge. Its initial objective had been to remove those who had deceived and misled the people of Japan to embark on world conquest. If we assume that it had been the militarists and ultranationalists who had misguided the Japanese, then the purge did successfully fulfill its mandate. These were the groups most heavily hit by the purge criteria and were the bulk of those removed.

Two diversely based analyses meshed to lend weight to the assumption that the primary aim in formulating purge policy should be the removal of the militarist and ultranationalist elites. First, Washington and SCAP policy makers could all agree that these groups had played the dominant role in shaping the aggressive policies of Japan. Furthermore, they were unanimous in viewing the militarists and ultranationalists as Japan's most dangerous leaders so far as the future peace of the world was concerned. These two groups, in the eyes of the foreign arbiters who controlled Japan's affairs, contained the vast majority of the "bad" Japanese who were willing to use terrorist tactics including genocide as a technique in subduing foreign and domestic rivals. To render Japan pacifist, therefore, these groups should no longer be allowed to contribute to the leadership of Japan. Second, Japanese government policy makers were perfectly willing to agree with this foreign assessment of those who had misled the people of Japan. They themselves were not sure; in fact, some of the participants in Japan's prewar and wartime administrations were vague as to how they had reached the decisions which led them to the brink of annihilation. So long as the alien conquerors restricted the blame to the militarists and ultranationalists for the destruction which Japan had spread on foreign soil, and which foreigners had spread in retaliation on the people and the countryside of Japan, other elites could expect to emerge from the Occupation era relatively unscathed. Hence, those leaders who were not drawn from these groups had everything to gain if they supported the analysis of the Occupation forces. Willing Japanese government compliance meshed neatly with the preconceived analysis of the Allied policy makers. It is readily understandable, therefore, that Japanese militarists and ultranationalists were saddled with the major share of responsibility for Japan's having challenged the peace of the world. Hence, in order to achieve the initial objective of making it impossible for Japan to do so again, these groups should be barred from exercising their authority and influence. This primary objective was successfully accomplished so long as the purge was enforced.

The purge was far less successful in aiding the development of a new, democratically inclined leadership in Japan. This secondary objective had been assigned to it, by indirection, in the initial press release explaining the purge. The basic weakness of the purge, which prevented it from completely fulfilling this mandate, lay in the purge criteria. These had been formulated on the assumption that Japan was to emerge with a pacifist, or at least nonaggressive leadership. Criteria formulated on this premise could not really be expected to achieve the removal of all Japanese who were potentially antidemocratic. (This idea itself is paradoxical as will be indicated.) Local leaders of the Imperial Rule societies and of the Ex-Servicemen's Association were purged, for example, in order to cleanse local government of reactionary elements whose presence would impede democratization. Yet the rationalization underlying the criteria remained frozen within the first objective, namely, that those responsible for Japan's militarist aggressions should be removed. The absurdity of linking these objectives became obvious once the purge was used against the Japanese Communist leaders. Most of them had spent the war years in jail because of their opposition to the Japanese war effort or had been abroad actively fighting (being traitors, if you will) against it. The relationship between the primary objective of the purge and the criteria implementing it, already strained in the expansion of the purge criteria to local levels of government, at this point became tenuous in the extreme. In the confusion of its objectives and in the ambiguity of expectations resulting from them lies the ultimate failure of the purge.

The purge criteria were premised on a rigid principle of guilt by association. The evidence consisted of having held a particular office, having espoused certain policies, or both. They were based, ostensibly, on the official position or policy orientation held during the era of Japanese expansion. This rationalization of the criteria was readily applicable to militarists and ultranationalists, but became less explicit as the purge moved into local government levels and into the economic and information media fields. By the time the purge criteria could be molded to encompass Communist leaders, this rationalization vanished into thin air. Substituted for it were the subjective views held by the formulators of the criteria of what constituted antidemocratic behavior or belief. Once this mixture was concocted, the purge floundered in a morass of contradiction and confusion.

Implementers of the purge also faced several knotty problems aside from reconciling the criteria with the conflicting objectives of the program. The administrative mechanism which enforced the purge was unwieldy. Control over the implementations of the program was not centralized initially in SCAP headquarters. By itself, this division of responsibility between two staff sections would not necessarily have mitigated against the success of the program. However, personnel in Government Section and in Civil Intelligence Section had differing responsibilities which affected their analyses of what the purge was to accomplish. In turn, this conflict exacerbated the problem of reconciling the contradictory objectives inherent in the purge program.

A second factor complicating the administration of the purge was the policy that all reforms were to be channeled through the existing structure of the Japanese government. This policy had several repercussions. It immeasurably slowed up the processes of formulating the criteria and of designating the purgees. Also it gave the Japanese government a means by which to protect domestic interest groups upon which it was dependent for political support. Moreover, the policy was not always adhered to by SCAP; this obscured the issue of who was responsible for actions taken in implementing the purge. Finally, a mammoth structure of screening committees came into existence, ostensibly to review the careers of public office holders and applicants for positions of authority. However, the *raison d'être* of these committees was open to question because of SCAP insistence—except when it wished to deviate therefrom—that the purge categories be rigidly applied. It was never clearly established whether Japanese committee members should use their own judgment or only utilize the purge criteria as the basis for their decisions. This latter approach had the advantages of limiting the power of the purgers and making more difficult the use of obstructionist tactics by Japanese officials. However, by being allowed discretion, screening committee members could have added an element of flexibility to interpreting the purge criteria. Conversely, the purge thereby could have become a capricious tool in the hands of purgers who might be unscrupulous power seekers. In the final analysis, emphasizing the categorical approach had the advantage of making it possible to utilize Japanese government institutions for implementation, important for the gaining of consent, without allowing the Japanese to use the purge as a political football.

Problems of surveillance over the activities of purgees were never effectively solved. The "undesirables" were designated, but this action by itself did not insure that their influence and authority were removed. In this respect, the Japanese purge differed drastically from those conducted in Nazi Germany or the Soviet Union. Incarceration, physical punishment, and outright liquidation were among the techniques employed in those countries as concomitants of a purge. In Japan, by contrast, the disabilities suffered by purgees were considerably less severe. Loss of status in public life, loss of pensions or other expected benefits, and loss of the right to pursue one's career inclinations, though serious enough, are not comparable to penal servitude or loss of life. The purge enforcers in Japan backed away from imposing those disabilities. Instead, they relied on political investigation agencies to track down purgees who had overstepped the complex legal limitations placed upon their activities. The whole arena of political affairs was thereby again opened for control by a reincarnation of the prewar thought-control police. (The influence of the reverse course in Occupation policy can again be noted in the transformation of the Japanese investigation organization, the original mission of which had been to supervise purgee activities.) Even without this shift in basic policy, however, a threat to the democratization objective was implicit in any agency investigating, and thereby controlling, the political activities of any individual or group.

Finally, the purge suffered from one other major weakness within the framework of the confusion inherent in the unrealistic objectives which had been assigned to it. Caution, guided by the need for maintaining social order, retarded and restrained its implementation. Concurrently, fear that a rapid removal of experienced leadership would result in "chaos, confusion, and communism" blunted the impact that the purge might have had.

An alternative approach would have been to implement the purge in one broad sweep. Several problems would have been faced had this approach been adopted. A basic prerequisite would have been that the policy makers have a clear understanding of their objectives. The speed of implementation would probably have resulted in a considerable number of unjustified removals. However, these injustices occurred anyway, in spite of the care employed and the time spent in formulating the purge criteria and processing the designations. (Individual injustices would probably be an inevitable concomitant to the utilization of categories as the basis for designations.) Furthermore, by speeding up the designation process, attention could have been turned much earlier to the correction of blanket applications of the purge criteria. Almost immediately, the Occupation could have established review agencies which would have considered the whole career of the appellant rather than just the purge criteria. A different frame of reference would thereby be provided within which the appellate machinery could operate to avoid duplicating the task of the screening agencies which emphasized the criteria as points of departure.

The alternative approach, emphasizing speed, would have had several inherent advantages. The purge would have had one solid impact, in contrast to its application in driblets which dissipated its shock potential. The speed of implementation would have lessened the confusion surrounding the issue of who was ineligible to hold public office in the new Japan. Also, those individuals who were not designated could have turned their energies more quickly to the task of rebuilding the ruins of the war without fear that an expansion of the purge might include them as well. The purge, no matter how timed, was a negative program. The sooner it could be completed, the sooner a concerted effort could be begun, with constructive rather than destructive objectives.

How the purge could have been made more effective has been the underlying theme of this analysis. Problems relative to the objectives of the program and to the purge criteria, alternative approaches to its implementation and to its timing, have been considered. In conclusion, attention will be turned to the fundamental problem. Did the purge have a role to play in relation to the over-all objectives of the Occupation: the democratization of Japan? If not, what alternatives might better have been utilized in the achievement of this major objective?

What were the dominant characteristics of the program as it was conducted? The purge reduced political behavior into rigid black and white categories; initially formulated on the basis of pro-war vs. antiwar attitudes, a prodemocratic vs. antidemocratic dichotomy was subsequently substituted for it. The task of a purge and of purgers is believed to be less difficult to the extent that the theory guiding these efforts assumes a stark "pro-anti" dichotomy of political orientation. To this extent, the purgers in Nazi Germany and in the Soviet Union who eliminated "enemies of the state or of the party" could do so with minimal pangs of conscience. To this extent also, the task of purgers professing a liberal democratic orientation is impossible because guilt by association is implicit in the use of this technique. Hence, the very tenets of political theory which liberal democracy assumes—freedom of speech, of assembly, of belief (no matter how far legal interpretations may limit them in actual practice)—are violated by creating a dichotomy of proponents and opponents.

If the foregoing is valid, the purgers constitute the most serious threat in using a purge to help transplant liberal democracy in alien soil. They cannot help arrogating unto themselves the determination of activities or beliefs which constitute behavior inimical to the new regime. Furthermore, the purgers can readily become addicted to the view that they can control public policy as well as manipulate leaders. As soon as a leader begins supporting policies which the purgers deem contrary to the interests of democratization, the purgers would determine that he should be removed. In Japan, for example, the purgers initially based removals on the activities of the individual in relation to policies of militarist aggression. In the end, the basis for removals was whether or not the individual was willing to restrict his political activities to tactics within the limits set by a parliamentary system of government.

Under these circumstances, should the purge have played any role in the Occupation of Japan? I would answer affirmatively if two qualifications are accepted. First, the purge should have been rapid. Second, the purge criteria should have been formulated with the objective of ridding Japan of its erstwhile leadership rather than obscuring the issue with criteria based on consideration of ostensible war guilt or antidemocratic activities and beliefs. By so "structuring" the purge, the assistance of the Japanese people could have been enlisted, for they too had suffered under the policies of their wartime leaders. Furthermore, the Occupation could have gained the coöperation of other Asian peoples who had felt the heel of Japanese imperialism. Viewed in this context, the purge would not have had to become involved in the democratization objective of the Occupation, with which it was clearly irreconcilable in theory.

Greater emphasis, of necessity, would have been given to other Occupation programs which were designed to bring about the democratization of Japan had the purge been restricted to ridding Japan of its existing leadership as rapidly as possible. The purge, under these circumstances, conceivably could have been more selective. By limiting the scope of the purge, the alien tutors of the Occupation would have had to exercise stricter controls; also these tutors would have had to play a much greater role in the shaping of domestic politics rather than being able to assume that because the "bad" Japanese had been removed, their replacements would take the responsibility for leading Japan onto the path of liberal democracy.

This alternative assumes that the purge and the task of democratization were theoretically incompatible; in addition, the Occupation should have given greater emphasis to two factors: (1) the fostering of a social and economic milieu within which liberal democracy could be expected to grow; (2) the utilization of reëducation on a far larger scale, until such time as the forces inherent in the "restructured" society could bring forth a new leadership. A basic prerequisite to such an effort would have been that Occupation personnel have a far greater degree of expert knowledge than they in fact did have, concerning Japanese society.

The key has not been found which might open the secrets to the manner in which the liberal democratic way of life (and its political, social, and economic institutions) might be transferred to societies in which it did not emerge as part of an indigenous process. The search conducted by the Occupation in Japan met with partial success. In the field of leadership, the purge did effectuate some changes; its impact could have been even greater. Its contribution to democratization was not impressive primarily because the purge as a concept proved antithetical to liberal democratic theory. For the achievement of democratization, greater success might have been possible if tutelage had played a larger role. Whatever the alternative, be it leadership change or reëducation, its implementers would sooner or later run into the Rousseauan paradox in which tutors ultimately force man to be free—or democratic.

BIBLIOGRAPHY

Allied Occupation and United States Government Official Documents and Reports

"Agreement of Foreign Ministers at Moscow on Establishing Far Eastern Commission and Allied Council for Japan," 27 December 1945, *PRJ*, Vol. II.

"Basic Initial Post-Surrender Directive to Supreme Commander for the Allied Powers for the Occupation and Control of Japan" (Joint Chiefs of Staff file number 1380/15, 3 November 1945). *PRJ*, Vol. II.

Far Eastern Commission. *Press Release* number 34, 10 July 1947.

Government Section, Supreme Commander for the Allied Powers. *Political Reorientation of Japan, September 1945 to September 1948.* 2 Vols. Washington, D.C., Government Printing Office, 1949.

Government Section, Supreme Commander for the Allied Powers, "Control of Anti-Democratic Elements," unpublished typescript of proposed supplement to *Political Reorientation of Japan*: "Removal of Ultranationalists" (n.d., but believed to have been prepared in 1951).

"History of the Purge," Government Section draft of "Removal of Ultranationalists." *PRJ*, Vol. I.

International Military Tribunal for the Far East. *Proceedings.*

MacArthur, Douglas. Comment on *Newsweek* article entitled, "Behind the Japanese Purge–American Military Rivalries," *PRJ*, Vol. II.

———. "Letter to Prime Minister Yoshida Shigeru," 1 November 1946. *PRJ*, Vol. II.

———. "Letter to Prime Minister Yoshida," 26 December 1946. *PRJ*, Vol. II.

———. "Letter to Prime Minister Yoshida Shigeru," 6 June 1950 (separate copy, mimeo.).

Montgomery, John D. *The Purge in Occupied Japan* (Technical Memorandum ORO-T-48 (FEC). Chevy Chase, Maryland: Johns Hopkins University (Operations Research Office), 1953. (Permission to cite this classified document granted by Brig. Gen. L. D. Flory (Ret.), Executive Director, Operations Research Office in letter dated 21 July, 1955.)

"Multilateral Treaty of Peace with Japan," *United States Treaties and Other International Agreements,* 1952, Vol. III, Part 3. Washington, D.C.: United States Government Printing Office, 1955.

Report of the Government Section to the Far Eastern Commission, 17 January 1946. General Headquarters, Supreme Commander for the Allied Powers (mimeo.), 1946.

SCAP. "Staff Memorandum No. 2," 21 January 1947. *PRJ*, Vol. II.

SCAPIN 93. "Removal of Restrictions on Political, Civil and Religious Liberties," *PRJ*, Vol. II.

SCAPIN 548. "Abolition of Certain Political Parties, Associations, Societies, and Other Organizations," 4 January 1946. *PRJ*, Vol. II.

SCAPIN 550. "Removal and Exclusion of Undesirable Personnel from Public Office," 4 January 1946. *PRJ*, Vol. II.

SCAPIN 919. "Removal and Exclusion of Diet Member," 3 May 1946. *PRJ*, Vol. II.

Supreme Commander for the Allied Powers, "Press Release concerning Purge Directives," 4 January 1946. *PRJ,* Vol. II.

"The Potsdam Declaration," *PRJ,* Vol. II.

"United States Initial Post-Surrender Policy for Japan." Prepared jointly by the United States Department of State, War Department, and Navy Department. *PRJ,* Vol. II.

Japanese Government

Official Documents and Reports

Cabinet Order No. 119, July 2, 1947. *PRJ,* Vol. II. Cf. also *Official Gazette* (Eng. ed.), Extra, 2 July 1947.

Cabinet Order No. 237, November 7, 1947. *PRJ,* Vol. I Cf. also *Official Gazette* (Eng. ed.), No. 482, 7 November 1947.

Cabinet Order No. 32, February 9, 1948. *Official Gazette* (Eng. ed.), No. 555, 9 February 1948.

Cabinet Order No. 145, July 1, 1948. *Official Gazette* (Eng. ed.), Extra No. 1, 1 July 1948.

Cabinet Order No. 39, February 8, 1949. *Official Gazette,* Extra No. 14 (Eng. ed.), 8 February 1949.

Cabinet Order No. 51, March 28, 1951. *Official Gazette,* No. 1499 (Eng. ed.), 28 March 1951.

Cabinet Order No. 220, June 18, 1951. *Official Gazette,* No. 1567 (Eng. ed.), 18 June 1951.

Cabinet Order No. 288, December 27, 1948. *PRJ,* Vol. II.

Cabinet Order No. 117, April 28, 1952. *Official Gazette* (Eng. ed.), Extra No. 43, 28 April 1952.

Cabinet and Home Ministry Ordinance No. 1, January 4, 1947. *PRJ,* Vol. II.

Cabinet and Ministry for Home Affairs Ordinance No. 2, February 28, 1947. *Official Gazette* (Eng. ed.), No. 273, 28 February 1947

Cabinet and Ministry for Home Affairs Ordinance No. 6, March 27, 1947. *Official Gazette* (Eng. ed.), No. 295, 27 March 1947.

Cabinet and Ministry for Home Affairs Ordinance No. 8, April 11, 1947. *Official Gazette* (Eng. ed.), No. 307, 11 April 1947.

Chuo Kōshoku Tekihi Shinsa Iinkai Jimukyoku (Central Public Office Qualifications Screening Committee Office), *Kōshoku Tsuihōrei no Kaisetsu* (*Expansion of the Public Office Purge Laws*) Fu: Kōshoku Kyoshokuin, Rōdo Tsuihō Kankei Hōrei Shu (Appendix: Collection of Laws concerning the Public Office, Educators, and Labor Purges). Tokyo, Zenkoku Chosonchokai Shuppanbu (National Town and Village Chiefs' Association Printing Bureau), 1947.

Imperial Ordinance No. 109, 28 February 1946 (separate copy, mimeo.).

Imperial Ordinance No. 346, 29 June 1946 (separate copy, mimeo.).

Imperial Ordinance No. 1, 4 January 1947. *PRJ,* Vol. II.

Imperial Ordinance No. 2, 4 January 1947. *PRJ,* Vol. II.

Imperial Ordinance No. 64, 3 March 1947. *PRJ,* Vol. II.

Imperial Ordinance No. 3, 4 January 1947. *PRJ,* Vol. II.

Imperial Ordinance No. 65 ("Appeals Procedure"), 1 March 1947. *PRJ,* Vol. II.

Imperial Ordinance No. 66, "Regulations on Organization of Public Office Qualifications Appeals Board," 1 March 1947. *PRJ,* Vol. II.

Imperial Ordinance No. 77, 12 March 1947. *PRJ*, Vol. II. Cf. also *Official Gazette* (Eng. ed.), No. 284, 13 March 1947.

"[Japanese] Government Announcement," *Press Release*, 13 January 1948, separate copy, mimeo. (Concerning screening Committee's decision to designate Hirano Rikizo as a purgee.)

Japanese Government, Ministry of Foreign Affairs. *Present Conditions of Japan: Political Section.* Tokyo, August, 1951.

Law No. 94, April 21, 1952. *Official Gazette* (Eng. ed.) No. 1822, 21 April 1952.

Law No. 193 "Law for the Establishment of the Attorney General's Office," 17 December 1947. *PRJ*, Vol. II.

Law No. 240 of 1952 (Subversive Activities Control Law), *Contemporary Japan*, Vol. XXI, 1952.

Naikaku (Cabinet), *Kōshoku Tekihi Shinsa Kijun Reiki Shu* (*Collection of Standards and Established Rules Concerning Public Office Qualification Screening*). Tokyo: (n.p., n.d.)

Prime Minister's Office and Ministry for Home Affairs Ordinance No. 4, July 2, 1947. *Official Gazette* (Eng. ed.), Extra, 2 July 1947.

Prime Minister's Office and Ministry for Home Affairs Ordinance No. 5, July 31, 1947. *Official Gazette* (Eng. ed.), No. 400, 31 July 1947.

Prime Minister's Office and Ministry for Home Affairs Ordinance No. 6, August 2, 1947. *Official Gazette* (Eng. ed.), No. 402, 2 August 1947.

Prime Minister's Office and Ministry for Home Affairs Ordinance No. 7, September 4, 1947. *Official Gazette* (Eng. ed.), No. 430, 4 September 1947.

Prime Minister's Office and Ministry for Home Affairs Ordinance No. 8, September 17, 1947. *Official Gazette* (Eng. ed.), No. 441, 17 September 1947.

Prime Minister's Office and Ministry for Home Affairs Ordinance No. 9, October 13, 1947. *Official Gazette* (Eng. ed.), No. 462, 13 October 1947.

Prime Minister's Office and Ministry for Home Affairs Ordinance No. 10, November 7, 1947. *Official Gazette* (Eng. ed.), No. 482, 7 November 1947.

Prime Minister's Office and Ministry for Home Affairs Ordinance No. 11, November 25, 1947. *Official Gazette* (Eng. ed.), No. 497, 25 November 1947.

Prime Minister's Office Ordinance No. 11, February 9, 1948. *PRJ*, Vol. II. Cf. also *Official Gazette* (Eng. ed.), No. 555, 9 February 1948.

Prime Minister's Office Ordinance No. 19, March 19, 1948. *Official Gazette* (Eng. ed.), No. 588, 19 March 1948.

Prime Minister's Office Ordinance No. 20, April 2, 1948. *Official Gazette* (Eng. ed.), No. 600, 2 April 1948.

Saiko Saibansho Jimu-Sokyoku Keijikyoku (Supreme Court, General Affairs Bureau, Prosecution Section), *Keiji Saiban Shiryō Dai Sanjuhachi Go: Kōshoku Tsuihō Kankei Jiken Hanketsu Shu* (*Criminal Court Records No. 38: Collection of Decisions of Cases connected with the Public Office Purge*), 1949.

———. No. 53, 1951.

Shugiin Giin Sosenkyo Kekka Shirabe (*Investigation of House of Representatives General Election Results*). Tokyo: Jichicho Senkyobu (Autonomy Agency Election Bureau), 1949, 1953, and 1955.

Shugiin Jimukyoku (House of Representatives Secretariat) *Shugiin Yoran* (*B*) (*House of Representatives Handbook*). Tokyo: Okurasho Shuppankyoku (Finance Ministry Printing Office), 1953.

"The Civil Code of Japan" (as amended by Law No. 222, 12 December 1947). *PRJ*, Vol. II.

"The Constitution of Japan." *PRJ*, Vol. II.

"The Development of Affairs concerning the Purge from Public Office," prepared by the Supervision Section of the [Japanese Government] Cabinet Secretariat, separate copy, mimeo., n.d.

Yoshida Shigeru, Prime Minister. "Letter to General Douglas MacArthur," October 31, 1946. *PRJ*, Vol. II.

Yoshida Shigeru, Prime Minister. "Letter to General Douglas MacArthur," December 21, 1946. *PRJ*, Vol. II.

Books

Ball, W. MacMahon. *Japan: Enemy or Ally?* Institute of Pacific Relations. New York: John Day Company, 1949.

Bisson, T. A. *Prospects for Democracy in Japan.* New York: Macmillan, 1949.

———. *Zaibatsu Dissolution in Japan.* University of California Press, 1954.

Brown, Delmer M. *Nationalism in Japan.* University of California Press, 1955.

Byrnes, James F. *Speaking Frankly.* New York: Harper and Brothers, 1947.

Cohen, Jerome B. *Japan's Economy in War and Reconstruction.* New York: Institute of Pacific Relations, 1949.

Coughlin, William J. *Conquered Press.* Palo Alto: Pacific Books, 1952.

Farley, Miriam S. *Aspects of Japan's Labor Problems.* New York: John Day Company, 1950.

Gayn, Mark. *Japan Diary.* New York: William Sloan Associates, 1948.

Grew, Joseph C. *Turbulent Era: A Diplomatic Record of Forty Years.* Ed. by Walter Johnson. Boston: Houghton Mifflin, 1952.

Kato Masuo. *The Lost War.* New York: A. A. Knopf, 1946.

Montgomery, John D. *Forced to be Free.* University of Chicago Press, 1957.

Scalapino, Robert A. *Democracy and the Party Movement in Prewar Japan.* University of California Press, 1953.

Stimson, Henry L. with McGeorge Bundy. *On Active Duty in Peace and War.* New York: Harper and Brothers, 1948.

Sumimoto Toshio, *Senryo Hiroku* (Hidden Materials Concerning the Occupation). 2 Vols. Tokyo: Mainichi Shimbunsha, 1952.

Tokyo Daigaku Shakai Kagaku Kenkyusho (Tokyo University Social Science Research Institute); Ukai Shinsei Project Chief, *Gyosei Iinkai* (*Administrative Committees*). Tokyo: Nippon Hyoronsha, 1951.

Truman, Harry S. *Memoirs: Year of Decisions.* Vol. I. New York: Doubleday, 1955.

Ueda Shunkichi and Takahashi Masumi. *Tsuihōsha no Undō no Genkai* (*Limits of Activities of Purgees*). Tokyo: Minori Shobosha, 1949.

Whitney, Major General Courtney. *MacArthur, His Rendezvous with History.* New York: A. A. Knopf, 1956.

Wildes, Harry Emerson. *Typhoon in Tokyo.* New York: Macmillan, 1954.

Monographs and Periodical Articles

Berkov, Robert H. "The Press in Postwar Japan," *Far Eastern Survey,* Vol. XVI, No. 14 (July 23), 1947.

Colton, Kenneth E. "Prewar Influence in Postwar Conservative Parties," *The American Political Science Review*, Vol. XLII, No. 5 (October, 1948).

Kauffmann, James Lee. "Report on Conditions in Japan" (mimeo.), 1947.

Kern, Harry J. "Trouble in Japan," *Newsweek*, Vol. XXIX, No. 25 (June 23, 1947).

Kinoshita Hanji. *Purge Policy and After*. Tokyo: Nihon Taiheiyō Mondai Chosakai (Japan Institute of Pacific Relations), 1954.

Kyogoku Junichi and Masumi Junnosuke. *Japanese Politics: Is it Democratized?* Tokyo: Nihon Taiheiyō Mondai Chosakai (Japan Institute of Pacific Relations), 1954.

MacArthur, Douglas. "Behind the Japanese Purge–American Military Rivalries," *Newsweek*, January 27, 1947.

Maruyama Masao. "Gunkoku Shihaisha no Seishin Keitai" (The Spiritual Structure of Military Leaders), *Chōryū* (*Current*), May, 1949.

Mainichi Shimbun (Mainichi Newspaper), 20 January 1948.

Oka Yoshisato. *Pattern of Power in Japanese Bureaucracy*. Tokyo: Nihon Taiheiyō Mondai Chosakai (Japan Institute of Pacific Relations), 1954. (Japan paper No. 7 for the Twelfth Conference of the Institute of Pacific Relations held in Kyoto, Japan, September–October, 1954.)

DATE DUE

MAY 21			
NOV 11 1969			
FEB 5 70-S			
JAN 17			
JAN 29			
MY 4 '81			
MY 5 '82			
MR 27 '83			
MY 2 '84			

GAYLORD PRINTED IN U.S.A.